FLYING CANADA

FIFTY YEARS OF FLYING THE NORTHLAND AND BEYOND

by Dr. Clair E. Schnupp

FLYING CANADA
FIFTY YEARS OF FLYING THE NORTHLAND AND BEYOND

by Dr. Clair E. Schnupp

Masthof Press
copyright © 2008

This title is available from:
Masthof Press
219 Mill Road
Morgantown, PA 19543-9516
Phone: 610-286-0258
email: mast@masthof.com
www.masthof.com

Cover photograph by Mark Petersheim.
Artwork by Matthew Troyer.

Library of Congress Control Number: 2008930985
International Standard Book Number: 978-1-60126-113-7

Published 2008 by
Masthof Press
219 Mill Road
Morgantown, PA 19543-9516

DEDICATION

I DEDICATE THIS BOOK TO
JAY WENDELL "WHITEY" HOSTETLER
OF RED LAKE SEAPLANE SERVICE
RED LAKE, ONTARIO, CANADA

I owe much to Whitey for his support throughout my flying experience. He helped me to acquire my original license in 1959. He also taught me many things about flying and caring for airplanes over the years, from the Piper J-3 to importing the Piper Cheyenne II in March, 2000. Thank you, Whitey.

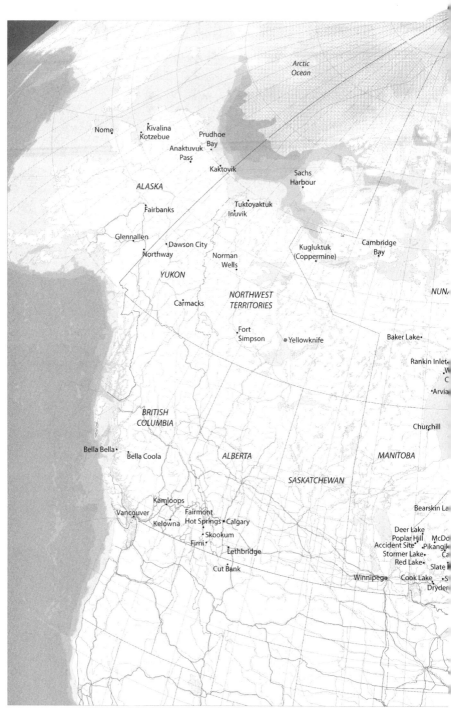

Upernavik•

KALAALLIT NUNAAT
(GREENLAND)

Ilulissat•

Sondre
Strømfjord•

•Iqaluit
Frobisher
Bay

NEW FOUNDLAND
AND LABRADOR

t Severn

out Lake
ake
w)

QUEBEC

ONTARIO
Lake
ut

NEW
BRUNSWICK
St. John•   *NOVA*
             SCOTIA

Ottawa • Montreal

Toronto

Canadä

CONTENTS

MAPS

Note: The maps are not to exact proportion. They are designed for general reference only.

ACKNOWLEDGEMENTS

First and foremost, I want to acknowledge my wife, **Clara,** for her belief in me and for her constant companionship through the half-century of my flying.

My **five daughters** have been a real part of my flying career. I thank them for their encouragement and hard work.

I want to acknowledge the late **George Lore** for his crude but well done flight training.

I want to acknowledge **Winnipeg Flying Club** for their excellent instrument flight training program.

I want to acknowledge **Mr. Chuck Bourne** for his patience in training me to fly the Piper Cheyene II properly, efficiently and safely.

I want to express a special thanks to all the good people at **Flight Safety International**, Lakeland, Florida, who have helped me annually to stay current in my flying through their recurrency program.

I am indebted to *The Sacred Romance* book by Brent Curtis and John Eldredge, for giving me a new picture of heaven. Some of my musings in the last chapter were inspired by their book.

I am grateful for **Matthew Troyer's** artistic abilities demonstrated in the pencil drawings for this book.

INTRODUCTION

For many years people have been asking me to write about my flying experiences. I flew out of necessity because of my career as a youth and family worker in Canada's northland and beyond. Flying was never the focus of my life; however, after I learned to fly I began to enjoy it and still do.

Now I have decided to respond to the requests and write some of my experiences to the best of my memory and from my perceptions. I trust you will find this book interesting, educational and inspiring.

These incidents took place during fifty years of flying over 12,000 hours in some of the harshest places and toughest conditions in Canada, Alaska, Central America, Panama and its off-shore islands, the Dominican Republic, Haiti and Greenland.

My wife, Clara, and our five daughters, Judy, Sharon, Carolyn, Cathie and Mary Lois, have been an invaluable part of my life. We were a family who lived, worked, played, flew, sang and prayed together.

Now my daughters are married. The pilot's training, flying and becoming nurses or teachers or counsellors is over. Our daughters have given Clara and me many grandchildren. I want to be a grandpa whom my grandchildren can admire. I want to leave a positive legacy for them to follow and this book is part of that legacy.

1

A BRUSH WITH DEATH

C rash!

My head banged against the aluminum dash of the little two-place Piper J-3 on skis. Everything went black. The date was December 10, 1962.

The temperature was -35°F when we crashed into the snow on a frozen lake on that wintery day. A friend and I were landing at a campsite to hunt moose, because moose meat was a staple part of our diet in northern Ontario, Canada.

The blackness enveloped me for a few moments before I regained consciousness. When I saw the light of day, I realized I was alive and my heart filled with joy and praise. Just as quickly, I turned to my passenger seated behind me. He looked okay. "Are you hurt?" I inquired anxiously.

"No," he assured me. He looked a bit nervous, but otherwise he was fine.

I assessed the situation. My head was fine and my thinking was normal, but it seemed that blood was everywhere. Red

was dripping down the front of my blue parka. The pain in my nose was intense and I was sure it was broken, but I decided that I could function with a broken nose.

To climb out of the wreckage and make a fire was imperative. I kicked the door open and crawled out and my passenger followed. We located the emergency box of food, the axe, matches and other necessary items.

We struggled through the deep snow toward the small trees on the shore and soon had a fire blazing. All of a sudden the reality hit me that we were alive! I began to cry loudly. My partner knew that my nose was injured, but he probably thought that my brain had been injured as well.

He ran over, grabbed me by the shoulders and started to shake me. "Are you okay? Are you okay? Are you okay?" he kept asking. Finally I was able to assure him that my sudden outburst of tears was because we were alive. Eventually I stopped crying, and he was reassured that I was all right.

Sure, my nose hurt badly! Big time! But the joy of having a sound mind and of being alive far outweighed the pain in my nose. Now that we had a fire and a cup of hot tea, we had some serious planning to do.

The accident happened at noon. Plans had been for me to pick up another fellow six miles away at another little camp by early afternoon. I had dropped him off in the morning.

My wife was expecting me to be home by 2 p.m. We had no radios in the little airplanes back in those days. I knew that by 2:30 or 3 p.m. my wife would become alarmed and would radio Whitey at Red Lake Seaplane Service to see if he could search for us in the morning. I also knew that she would be worried throughout the long winter night.

It was a long winter night. I remember catching up on hours of ironing and mending because sleep had left me. My imagination was running wild; accident; the men freezing; me left with two little girls. I would pray. I would call on the ham radio. Finally in the early morning, I reached Whitey.
– Clara

My passenger and I did some calculations and concluded that around ten o'clock the next morning a plane would be searching for us. Smoke signals were our only way of communicating. We knew that pine needles had a large amount of tar in them and that when put on a campfire, they ignite quickly, sending billows of smoke into the sky. By morning we would need to have a huge pile of pine branches next to our campfire.

For the present we needed food and then we needed to walk the six miles to the other man I had dropped off that morning. The three of us would need to walk back, so we wanted to do as much of the walking in the daylight as possible. We had a good map and knew the moon would be out on a clear night. We melted snow for water to cook some dried soup which tasted good and refreshed us. Then we headed off for our twelve-mile trek to bring the other man to our camp.

We knew that it was never a good idea to leave a crashed airplane, since an airplane is easier for search parties to see than a person. We wanted to camp close to the airplane for the night.

By 6:30 p.m. we had the tiring trek behind us. All three of us were back at the camp close to the wrecked airplane.

After cooking more dried soup and drinking more black tea, we made a place to put our sleeping bags for the long night by packing down the snow and putting pine branches on top of the snow for a nice "mattress." Then we rolled out the sleeping bags and took turns sleeping and caring for the fire.

When morning finally came, my nose had stopped bleeding, but the front of my parka was covered with a thick layer of dried blood. We cooked rolled oats for breakfast and made black tea. Also, we needed to make a pile of pine branches close to the campfire no later than 9:30 a.m.

At 9:50 a.m. we heard the sound of an airplane in the distance. We quickly put all the pine branches on the fire. A huge column of smoke soared up into the sky. We were spotted! We were excited because an airplane was coming to pick us up.

The excitement didn't last long. The airplane was on a track from Red Lake to Deer Lake, Ontario, which put it

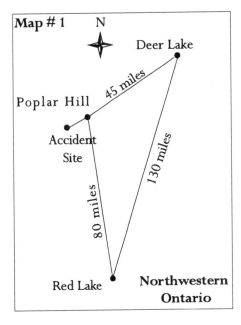

Map # 1

N

Deer Lake

Poplar Hill

45 miles

Accident Site

130 miles

80 miles

Red Lake

Northwestern Ontario

too far to the east to see us.

As the drone of the airplane faded, so did our spirits. We quickly cut some more pine branches, but before we had very many cut, we heard the sound of another airplane. As we put the pine branches we had collected on the fire, a smaller column of smoke soared up into the sky. The airplane turned towards us and was soon overhead.

Whitey had come with a Cessna 180. As he landed, we gathered up our things for our ten-minute flight back home. The Cessna 180 ski plane taxied right up to us, making it easier to load our gear and climb aboard. We were thankful to be alive and on our way home.

Landing back home on the snow-covered lake, we taxied up near the dock where my wife and others were waiting to meet us. When Clara saw all of us and the blood caked on the front of my parka, she knew we had had an airplane accident and survived! She had always been so fearful about flying. Knowing that we had an accident and were alive and well gave her some release from her fear.

After greeting everyone who was there, I went along with Whitey to Red Lake to have my nose examined. After the examination the doctor said, "Your nose is broken and crooked, but it will heal and be fine." I wanted to have my nose straightened. The doctor showed me his crooked nose from a car accident and asked, "Why go through an operation when you look fine?" I was satisfied with his obvious opinion, and so my nose is crooked to this day.

Later, I learned what else had happened the day of the accident. My close childhood friend was going from the barn to the house for lunch when a voice said, "Pray for Clair." He told me later that he went back into the barn and prayed specifically for me over 1500 miles away! God moves in mysterious ways to care for His own.

What caused the accident? There is a saying that the accident rate is higher around 200 hours of flying and again around 1000 hours of flying. I had 196 hours. Being a Type A personality, I was over-confident and had some lessons to learn the hard way.

I had wanted to make a quiet landing that would not require much taxiing to the campsite, so I was landing too low and too slow in a slideslip. Because I was just above stalling speed, the left wing stalled and, consequently, we crashed into the snow and ice with a big bang. There was a considerable amount of damage to the aircraft. The crash scared away any potential moose, but moose meat was no longer important. It is amazing how quickly one's priorities can be rearranged.

Whitey was not too pleased with me and I could understand why. He gave me a few more hours of dual instruction for which I was very grateful.

The following summer the airplane was taken apart and hauled by canoe on the Berens River to the end of the road at Berens Landing. Later it was taken to Red Lake Seaplane Service and repaired.

Life Lesson GOD AND WHITEY TAUGHT ME SOME NECESSARY LESSONS ABOUT OVER-CONFIDENCE. GOD ALSO TAUGHT ME THAT HE DOES CARE FOR ME EVEN IN MY MISTAKES.

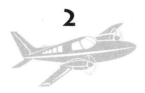

2

LEARNING TO FLY

Backtracking a bit, I want to tell you why I learned to fly.

"Clair, would you come into my office?" asked Irwin Schantz, the director of the organization of my employment at Red Lake, Ontario.

I groaned inwardly, *What have I done wrong this time?* I carried a fear of failure from my childhood.

During World War II, my father was gone for three formative years of my life. I have no memories of those years except the scary dreams of Hitler's bombers dropping bombs on us. My father's absence and the fear of Hitler's bombs created an insecurity, an anxiety and I carried a fear of failure until thirty years of age, when Dr. Clyde Narramore helped me work through my childhood experiences.

I entered Irwin's office and took a chair. He began by saying, "If you had your pilot's license, you could come and go as necessary."

"I never considered that before," I replied, "but since we live eighty miles north of Red Lake for our youth work, I can see that it would be beneficial. As a farm boy I never thought about getting a pilot's license, but it does make sense to me to pursue pilot's training."

"Well," he said, "what do you think of this plan? You pay for the gas, I'll provide a Piper J-3, and George Lore will teach you to fly. Whitey will arrange things and help you along the way."

"Sounds great to me," was my immediate response.

In September, 1959, Whitey and I went to Baudette, Minnesota, where my flying experiences began. George Lore had been a military instructor during World War II, so instructing was in his blood. George was a good instructor.

If the nose of the plane was too high, he would slap the dash and say in a harsh voice, "Get that _____ _____ nose down!" Believe me, I got that nose down. His methods were rough, but he taught me to fly—crosswind landings, short field landings, partial stalls, full stalls, spins and all the other necessary procedures he believed to be important for bush flying.

George even taught me special emergency procedures, since I was going to be a bush pilot. One day he told me, "We will do spins with the floats on." He advised me that it was not a procedure recommended by most instructors, but he felt I needed to know how to recover from a spin because it could be done safely.

"You will be flying on floats a lot and I want to teach you to be as safe as possible," he said.

"Sounds good to me. If I'm going to fly, I want to do it as safely as possible," I responded nervously.

I learned to do spins with floats. I practised them over Lake of the Woods and it was fun, even though at first I was a little scared.

One day when I walked into George's office he said, "Give me your Student License and let me sign it. It will be your temporary Private Pilot's License until the other one comes in the mail. We planned to do your test flight today, but I have been watching you fly around here on wheels and floats. The other day I saw you practising takeoffs on floats in a circle here on Rainy River. You sure handle that plane well. I knew you were practising takeoffs and climb-outs in a circle so you would know how to do it if you ever got stuck on a very small lake."

"That's true," I said.

He went on to say, "Also, the last few times we flew together, I was testing you in different ways such as taking away your power." He was referring to pulling the throttle back and holding it while I did a "dead-stick" landing on floats.

He continued, "I remember before you flew on floats you were on your first cross-country flight when the airplane lost oil pressure. You landed in a farmer's field. You found that I accidently forgot to put on the oil cap. You bought motor oil from the farmer and flew back here to the airport. That was good doings, young man."

George signed my license and said, "This license, you know, is only a 'permit' to go out there and learn to fly through experience over the next few years."

Away I flew to Red Lake.

One year later I wrote my Canadian exam and obtained my Canadian Pilot's License.

I liked George Lore in spite of his crude manners and language. I think that George Lore liked me too. He believed in me and liked what I was doing for youth. George helped to fill some of the vacuum left in little Clair's heart when his daddy was gone for three years during World War II. I never saw George after he signed my license, because I was always up North. About ten years later I heard that George was killed in an airplane accident. I never did hear the details, but hearing of his death saddened me. George is dead, yet the memories live on in my heart and flying.

During the next few years I learned much about flying in the bush country of northern Ontario. I remember one hot summer evening when there was absolutely no wind. The lake was as smooth as glass. I filled both gas tanks and helped my passenger into the plane. Then I loaded our two briefcases and two overnight bags.

I taxied out to the other side of the lake to take off. The airplane would not take off because there was not much lift, so I returned to the dock. We took the not-so-essentials out of our two briefcases and night bags. We packed the essentials into one briefcase and one night bag. We pumped every drop of water that we could out of the floats and taxied out again.

That made the difference on that hot, calm summer evening. On the takeoff I was able to lift one float first and seconds

later the other float, and away we went. As we were climb-
ing out, I remembered something that Whitey often told me.
If a pilot tries long enough to take off on the water, he will
eventually use up enough fuel that he will be able to take off.
Whitey also warned me to let the engine have time to cool
down between aborted takeoff runs. Otherwise the engine becomes severely overheated and damaged. Some pilots even had
accidents due to engine failure after takeoff and before they had
enough altitude to set up properly for an emergency landing.

Life Lesson FLYING ON FLOATS HAS
TAUGHT ME TO KEEP LIFE
SIMPLE. WHEN WE COLLECT TOO MUCH PERIPHERAL
STUFF, WE BECOME EMOTIONALLY OVERLOADED AND
LIFE BECOMES BURDENSOME. THE SCHEDULE BECOMES
TOO FULL. WE CAN EASILY END UP WITH AN EMOTIONAL
OVERLOAD. THE FREEDOM TO "FLY" IS GONE! WE NEED TO
CONSTANTLY EVALUATE HOW MUCH WE DO AND BUY.

Then there was learning how to take care of the airplane
in the wintertime. During the long winter night, a pilot has to
cover the engine well with a quilted nose cover to keep the engine warm. With a Coleman catalytic heater inside the cowling
and the quilted engine cover, the engine could be kept warm.

I remember one Christmas season when Clara and I vis-
ited young people in a number of communities. It was a cold
trip, but we had some very positive times with the youth and

their families. After five days, we headed home. Clara had a blanket over her knees and was holding the Coleman catalytic heater to keep warm.

This heater really helped. Sitting in the Piper J-3 for a two-hour flight without it was COLD.
– Clara

After we arrived we parked the plane, on skis of course, just below our house so we could keep an eye on it. Suddenly, someone screamed, "The airplane is on fire!" Several of us went out with fire extinguishers and put out the fire. Some of the cockpit was burnt, especially overhead where the fabric was.

Upon investigation, we discovered that after Clara had climbed out, she placed the Coleman catalytic heater on her seat and put the blanket on top of the heater. We had been cold and tired from the trip and overlooked the danger the heater and blanket posed.

What a relief this was for me. I felt so responsible.
– Clara

The next morning I radioed Whitey and told him what had happened. He and another pilot came in to examine the damage. There was no structural damage, just ruined fabric on the top of the cockpit.

Whitey asked for a bed sheet and two buckets of water. I wondered what a bed sheet and two buckets of water would do, but I brought what he requested.

"In the -30°F temperatures," Whitey said, "I'll put the bed sheet over the burnt fabric. I'll pour water over the bed sheet and freeze it to the good fabric. This bed sheet will make a cover over the hole in the top of the cockpit."

"Smart idea," I replied. "It sure won't melt in flight at this frigid temperature."

When the temporary fix was finished, Whitey flew the airplane to Red Lake. Later, in the hangar, the burnt fabric was replaced and everything restored to normal. In a few days the airplane was back in the air, and we were all the wiser. Pilots appreciate good mechanics who know what they are doing.

•　　•　　•

Slush is another big problem in winter flying. There are places where the weight of the snow will push the ice down, then water comes up through the cracks. This water is covered with a thick blanket of soft snow which keeps the water between the thick cover of snow and the ice from freezing. This forms the slush.

Slush is one of the worst enemies of a bush pilot flying a ski plane. The pilot must learn where the slush might be. If he is landing or taxiing and encounters slush, he must keep moving as fast as possible to move beyond where the slush is.

Late one afternoon my fourteen-year-old daughter, Judy, and I were flying from Red Lake, Ontario, to Pickle Lake. This trip took us over the community of Slate Falls. Just past Slate Falls it began to snow. The snow became thicker so we were following the power line to Pickle Lake. We were only about twenty miles from Pickle Lake when the snow reduced visibility to one-half mile.

We were over the shoreline of a large lake that ran along the power line when I spotted an abandoned building and pulled back the throttle. I landed straight ahead on the lake along the shoreline. When a pilot is landing on a snow-covered lake in snowing conditions, the shoreline provides the depth perception for a safe landing.

As I was touching down, I saw deep fluffy snow and immediately thought of slush. As the airplane settled down, I could see the skis go down through the fluffy snow and the slush rush up over the skis. The plane came to a quick stop. There was no time to "give it power" and move beyond the slush.

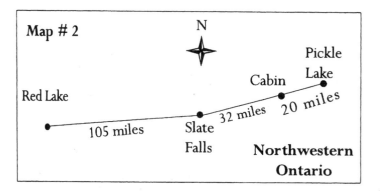

"Well, Judy, I think we are stuck for the night," I said with a sinking feeling. I continued, "There is a cabin just behind us on the right side along the shore."

Darkness was coming fast and the snow was thickening. I took out the axe before we worked our way to the shore and to the abandoned house. It was a place to sleep, but before we could take anything out of the plane to eat or sleep, we had to cut down some young trees for poles to pry up the skis. We needed to put poles under the skis before they froze into the slush. All the while we had to keep our feet from becoming too wet because of the cold temperature.

About midnight we had the skis up on poles lying cross ways under them. Then, with homemade snowshoes, we had to tramp the snow into the slush ahead of the airplane so it could freeze and serve as a "runway" the next morning to take off.

By 1:30 a.m., a fire was crackling in an old barrel stove. I quickly checked to see if our feet were frozen. It was a relief when I saw that they were not frozen and white; they were only very cold and pink. Then we had something to eat and settled down for some sleep because we were completely exhausted.

The next morning the sky was clear. I had put the catalytic heater under the cowling and had put on the nose cover sometime during the whole ordeal the evening before. At the crack of dawn we were off to Pickle Lake. There we could rest, relax and eat before continuing on our journey.

This was a bonding experience for a father and his fourteen-year-old daughter. We had what it took to do the job and survive the night.

Yes, I was still learning to fly in all types of conditions! George Lore knew what he meant when he had said, "Now go and learn to fly."

Following is a diary entry Judy wrote of flying with me:

When we sat belted into that enclosed space, especially during an uneventful flight that extended into dusk, with the drone of the engine and the crackle of the HF radio, a cozy cocoon was created that stayed with me through the years. On the other side of the coin, during flights with low ceilings and visibility limited by snow, I have good memories of watching Dad sit alert and leaning forward, his map wrapped into a tight bundle around our current route, his eyes moving back and forth between the blue line on his map and curves of lake shore, peering out to identify our moment by moment position, as well as possible landing options, and continually assessing weather conditions, his whole being crackling with intensity.

3

A BUSH PILOT

Bang! A strange sound came from the motor of the two-place float plane that a friend and I were flying. I pulled the throttle immediately and turned off the ignition. When the motor stopped, everything was deathly quiet.

All those times when George Lore "cut the throttle" to teach me "dead-stick" landings rushed into my mind. I was flying on floats and there was a big lake underneath us. The whole lake was a runway.

In the back of my mind I could hear George saying, "Relax, drop the nose, keep up that gliding speed until you are ready to flare out for the landing. Land as slowly as possible, regardless of what you might be landing on."

I did exactly as I had been taught. Within twelve seconds we were sitting quietly on the lake. My passenger and I looked at each other in shock, disbelief and relief!

"We are down safely, but we are miles from any community," I said to my passenger.

"Where are we?" he asked.

I looked carefully at the map and said, "We are on the north end of McDowell Lake. This is a large lake with many inlets, islands and large bays."

"Does anyone live near here?" he asked.

"Yes, there is a small settlement on the southern part of this huge lake. But we have no radio to communicate with them, or anyone else, for that matter," I replied.

He prayed, "Oh God, help someone in a boat or an airplane to spot us."

"Amen," I agreed.

Meanwhile we decided to find the small tool kit. We stood on the floats and removed the cowlings. It is not the easiest thing to do when the airplane is bobbing up and down with the waves. We carefully put the cowling inside the airplane. We were careful to put every screw, nut and bolt inside the airplane, one piece at a time, as we removed them.

As untrained mechanics, our challenge was to determine what the damage was. We wanted to have some idea of what had gone wrong, so we would know what to say on the radio in the morning if someone found us.

Externally the engine looked to be in perfect condition. We removed the four spark plugs to determine if all four cylinders had compression. Well, one did not. We looked in with a little flashlight and saw a hole in the piston.

"This piston has a hole," I shouted above the noise of the water splashing against the floats.

"I know we can't fix that," my passenger said. I heartily agreed.

We knew that we needed one cylinder and piston assembly replacement unit. The whole episode could have been much worse, yet we were miles from anyone.

By now the wind was moving us toward the south shore of the large north bay on McDowell Lake. We realized that in another thirty minutes we would be at the shore. We had plenty of ropes and emergency supplies along.

Just then we heard the sound of a boat motor far in the distance. We saw that the boat was coming our way. We were thankful, very thankful.

When the boat arrived, we slowly pulled it alongside the float and held the boat by the rim. I recognized the man in the boat. We had done some youth work together a few years before. He was my interpreter on occasion. I had seen him and his wife at Beaver Lake Camp at Dryden, Ontario, several times.

"Thanks a million for checking on us, Albert. I didn't realize you were around," I exclaimed.

"What's your problem?" he asked.

"Got a hole in the piston," I told him. "Does the HF radio work at your house?" I asked.

"It sure does, but the signals won't be good until morning," he informed me. He continued, "But I can pull you to shore. Got any long ropes?"

"Sure do," I said as I pulled out a twenty-five-foot rope. I tied it to the front of the floats. I tossed Albert the other end. He caught it and tied it to his boat.

"You can pull us to shore by a flat rock if you can find one," I said.

"I know exactly the spot to tie up the airplane for the night," he informed me.

As we were going to shore, I had to think about how well these people know their country.

Later Albert told us that he had heard the sound of a plane but the sound had disappeared. He thought the plane was gone on its journey to its destination, but soon he noticed a little plane far off in the distance. He decided he would check out what was happening. I thought, *How considerate.*

We were relieved and thankful that he came and pulled the airplane to the shore. When we arrived at the shore, we carefully secured the plane for the night. Albert found three strong trees to which we tied the three ropes we had along.

After gathering our necessities for the night, we went with Albert to his small settlement. He provided a place for us to sleep after his wife, Ida, fixed us some fish for supper. We were hungry, to say the least.

The next morning, after some black tea and bannock (Indian bread), I called Whitey at Red Lake on the radio phone and explained the trouble. He said he would send an airplane that morning with Ned Graber, one of his mechanics. Whitey had a spare replacement cylinder unit in stock for that particular motor for which we were very thankful.

By 10:30 a.m. the airplane had arrived with Ned and the parts. Four hours later we were on our way, and Ned was on his way back to Red Lake.

Life Lesson THE KINDNESS AND HOSPITALITY OF THE PEOPLE IN THE NORTH REMINDS ME OF THE INNATE CONCERN PEOPLE DO HAVE FOR ONE ANOTHER. GOD HAS CREATED US WITH A SENSE OF COMPASSION FOR OTHERS, BUT IN THE NOISE AND RUSH OF URBAN LIFE, PEOPLE TEND TO BE PREOCCUPIED WITH THEMSELVES AND THEIR OWN PROBLEMS, AND THEY OFTEN DO NOT NOTICE PEOPLE IN NEED.

•   •   •

By this time I was flying a six-place Cessna 206. The hydraulic skis were ordered but had not yet arrived. The Tom

Zeager family came to Beaver Lake for a visit. It was January and frigid.

Tom and his family were interested in a visit to Round Lake. The next morning the weather was good so we packed what we needed for the day and went over to the airport. After checking the plane over and filing a flight plan, we were on our way to Round Lake. We spent several hours there. On the way home Tom wanted to stop at Pickle Lake to visit someone he knew. While Tom and his family were visiting, I was doing practise circuits since the 206 was rather new for me. I was practising short landings between the end of the runway and the exit taxiway. Eventually I had perfected the proper approach and landing speeds for short field landings that were given in the Pilot's Handbook.

I could have been drinking coffee during Tom's visit, but God knew I would need the extra practise. Only He knew what would happen on the flight home on wheels in winter time.

Within one and a half hours we started our trip from Pickle Lake to Dryden Municipal Airport. I had phoned my wife from Pickle Lake to give her our ETA (estimated time of arrival). She was at the Dryden airport a little ahead of time and was talking with the radio operator when I called in fifteen miles north of the airport to report my position and revised ETA.

We were all excited that a good day was nearly over. I had just finished my landing checks when everything up front began clattering and banging. Smoke was pouring out of the engine! The engine stopped immediately. The propeller stood still in a straight up and down position. My altitude was about 2500 feet, and below us was a winding gravel road and a nice little lake.

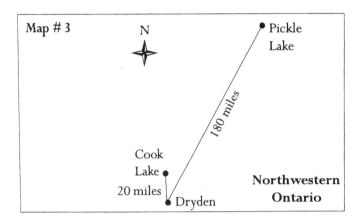

Again, everything George Lore taught me about "deadstick" landings rushed into my mind. That, along with the experience I was acquiring, all came together. Land on wheels in three feet of snow on the frozen lake? Yes, lower the nose, keep a good glide speed until flareout for landing.

The snow was deep, so there was the reality that the nose wheel could break off, and if it did there would be damage to the airplane. Tom and Helen were in the back two seats because they had wanted to talk. *That's good*, I thought. *They are the biggest. There needs to be as much weight as possible in the back so I can flareout and land as slowly as possible. I need to hold the nose wheel up as long as possible.* I remembered everything I had learned just one and a half hours earlier while doing my circuits at Pickle Lake.

At 1000 feet I calculated that there was sufficient weight in the back for a light, nose-wheel landing. I was lined up for

a dead-stick landing on Cook Lake, a lake I knew well from family fishing trips. I called on the radio, "Mayday. Mayday. Motor quit. Landing on Cook Lake. Send another airplane."

In the airport, my wife's heart did a flip. The radio operator's voice came over the radio, "Yes, C-FZNS, we copy and will send someone just as soon as possible."

By now I was on my flareout. Just as the two main wheels touched the snow, I pulled back on the yoke as hard as I could. The nose stayed up and the main gear did a nice slide in the deep snow as the nose wheel touched the snow and the airplane came to a complete stop on all three wheels. Later, as we looked at the tracks in the snow, we saw that the tail cone actually touched first and then the two main wheels. The nose wheel mark in the snow was very short.

It was all over. Everything was very quiet and there was no fire. Finally Tom said, "Praise the Lord!" I agreed.

Soon a small two-place Cessna 152 was circling over-head. We talked on the radios and I told him we were all safe. He said, "A Beaver ski plane is preparing to come for you." We were all relieved. He reported to the Dryden airport radio operator that everyone was fine.

That night, around our dining table, there was much talking, laughing with re-lief and expressing thankfulness for safety.

What a relief for me!
– Clara

The mechanics were able to acquire a caterpillar tractor and wagon. They went out to Cook Lake, loaded the Cessna 206 on the wagon, and hauled it to a friend's farm a few miles away. There it was put into the barn for the mechanics to do their work.

The motor was damaged beyond repair, because a main bearing had gone out. The connecting rod broke and went through the side of the crank case. This allowed the oil to flow out onto the hot exhaust pipe, causing all the smoke. Thankfully, there was no fire!

Within a few days the replacement motor came and was installed. I did a test flight and all checked out well. The hy-draulic wheel-skis arrived too and they were installed. It was a happy ending to what otherwise could have been a tragedy.

• • •

The next summer I was visiting a remote community while flying the Luscombe 8F on floats. I had finished a good visit and planned to go to another community even though there was a strong wind.

I assessed the situation and knew that I could take off back in the bay away from the big waves with their white caps. I pumped the water from the floats and did the other necessary checks.

During my flight training, Whitey had told me always to taxi on floats with the doors unlatched, especially if it is windy. From experience he had learned that if the wind is stronger than the pilot estimated and began to lift one wing, the pilot or the passenger could jump out on the float and hang on the strut. The strut goes from the belly of the airplane to the centre of the bottom of the wing.

As I was taxiing out to the bay, I realized that the wind was stronger than I had estimated. Suddenly, the right wing was being lifted too high by the cross wind.

Judy, in the right seat, was a good swimmer and had little fear of water. I yelled, "Judy, jump out on the float and hang on to the wing strut!" Judy did just that as I gave the engine power until the plane was more level. Judy's hair was blowing in the prop wash, but her weight helped to level the plane. Then I shut off the engine which allowed the plane to weathervane with the nose into the wind. That way it would stay straight and level except for the bobbing up and down in the huge waves. Judy crawled back into the plane, glad to be out of the wind.

"That was a scary one, wasn't it?" I said.

"Yeah," Judy agreed.

Judy and I looked at each other as our adrenaline subsided. We let the wind take us to whatever shore it would. We each readied a rope. In about seven minutes we approached a flat rock and I jumped off the back of the float onto the rock to steady the plane tail first on the shore.

No one from the community noticed what happened. After about five hours the wind began to subside in the early evening. We taxied back to the community for something to eat before we continued our trip.

Life Lesson   *I DID AS I WAS INSTRUCTED TO DO IF CAUGHT IN A STRONG SIDE WIND WHILE TAXIING ON THE WATER. IT WORKED. LIFE JUST WORKS MUCH BETTER IF WE DO THE RIGHT THINGS WE HAVE BEEN TAUGHT TO DO, ESPECIALLY IF WE DO WHAT GOD'S WORD TELLS US TO DO.*

•   •   •

Another time my daughter, Sharon, was flying with me on a trip. She was in the right-hand seat. I was going to visit some youth up North. We were in the Luscombe 8F on floats. As the two-hour flight continued, I realized that there was more headwind than I had anticipated. I had plenty of fuel, but with the extra time it was taking we were running out of daylight.

Although the weather was forecasted to be clear all day, thirty minutes from our destination we came under a heavy cloud layer. The sunlight began to disappear rapidly. I could see it would be impossible to reach my destination by dark. No other communities were closer.

The only right option was to land as soon as possible and set up camp before darkness overtook us.

I told Sharon, "We could probably arrive at our destination, but with the headwinds and this unexpected cloud cover, I am going to land on this lake right below us. It is better to be sure we can camp here alive than hope we reach our destination alive." She agreed, trusting her father's decisions.

> *Life Lesson* GOD EXPECTS US TO USE OUR HEADS. *I* ALWAYS FLY WITH THREE, OR NO FEWER THAN TWO, ALTERNATIVES OR OPTIONS. WHEN *I* AM DOWN TO ONE OPTION, *I* TAKE IT. WHEN A PILOT IS IN THE AIR AND CLOSES OFF ALL OPTIONS EXCEPT THE "*I* MUST ARRIVE AT ALL COSTS" OPTION, IT MOST LIKELY WILL COST THE PILOT MUCH MORE THAN HE IS EXPECTING.

We landed. To our surprise, the entire lakeshore was swamp. We taxied around until we found one flat rock and a few trees. The area was large enough for a campfire and sleeping bags. Every seasoned bush pilot should have plenty of mosquito repellent and/or mosquito netting along to survive a night, and we did.

We cooked a supper of dried soup and had some black tea with sugar. After putting more wood on the fire, we rolled out our sleeping bags for a good sleep.

The next morning was clear and calm. After some rolled oats and black tea for breakfast, we packed up our gear and arrived at our destination without incident. I was becoming a more seasoned bush pilot with every new experience. I was still learning to fly as George Lore had told me to do.

Life Lesson I BELIEVE THAT GOD WILL HELP US WHEN WE DO OUR PART. MY FATHER ALWAYS SAID, "DO YOUR BEST AND GOD WILL DO THE REST, BUT IF YOU DON'T DO YOUR BEST, GOD MAY VERY WELL NOT DO THE REST."

• • •

One spring I had been flying frequently in the far northern part of Ontario. It was a warm spring day as I flew south to Red Lake to have some mechanical work done at Red Lake Seaplane Service.

It never dawned on me that it may have been warmer farther south. I landed closer to the hangar side of the lake where the snow had not been packed.

As I landed the Luscombe 8F (a taildragger), I could feel the front two skis being pulled into the deep, wet, sticky snow. Then just as the airplane nearly stopped, the tail came up and the airplane was standing on its nose.

To say the least, I felt very embarrassed, because I knew many people could see my airplane in that awkward position. All I could see was snow and a bent propeller.

The mechanics took the airplane into the hangar and did the necessary inspections. The propeller was sent off to be straightened. Fortunately Red Lake Seaplane Service had a spare that I could use in the meantime. Also I had to find a quiet place to let my adrenaline settle and to reflect on what I could learn from this experience.

Life Lesson   *I KNEW I WOULD THINK MORE CARE-FULLY WHEN SPRING COMES AND AT WHAT LATITUDE I AM LANDING ON SKIS. I WAS STILL LEARNING SOME MORE LESSONS ABOUT BUSH FLYING. LEARNING TO BECOME A BUSH PILOT IS MORE INVOLVED THAN BECOMING A PRIVATE PILOT FLYING IN AND OUT OF AIRPORTS. LEARNING IS A NEVER-ENDING EXPERIENCE. THE SAME APPLIES TO GOD, WHO WANTS US TO KEEP LEARNING FROM THE BIBLE, SO WE CAN MAKE WISE DECISIONS IN THIS JOURNEY OF LIFE.*

4

EMERGENCIES

One long hot summer day I had been visiting youth in various communities. At sunset I arrived at Round Lake, Ontario. I taxied to the beach in front of Rev. Bert Brown's house. As my plane moved close to the beach, I turned off the engine and climbed out on the float as the airplane slowly drifted to the sandy beach.

"Hi, Bert, a nice summer evening, eh?" I called out.

Bert's reply was very subdued as he answered, "Yes, it is."

Bert helped turn the airplane around and we both pulled the plane tail first onto the beach. I tied a long rope from the tail ring to a big tree.

As we stood on the beach in the cool of the evening, everything was quiet and peaceful. The last faint glow of a beautiful sunset slowly diminished, but Bert seemed very concerned about something. I studied his mood.

"Bert," I said, "is something troubling you?"

His reply was, "Yes, my eight-year-old daughter is very

sick. The medicine the nurses gave her is not helping, so they want to send her to the hospital. You know there is not an airport here yet, so we can't get a medivac plane to take her out." We slowly walked to the house. Upon entering the house, I could see his little girl was very pale, weak and sick. Bert said helplessly, "I hope she lives till morning."

I pondered the whole situation and began to do some calculations. *With the full moon glistening on the lakes on a clear night, I could safely fly her to the Red Lake hospital,* I thought to myself.

"Bert, do you have a flashlight?" I asked. *A flashlight would help me to see the map,* I thought.

"Yes," was his reply.

"Would you like for me to fly her out tonight to the Red Lake hospital?" I offered.

"If you feel you can, I would really appreciate it," was his response.

"I am sure I can," I replied.

We agreed that I would do the flight. He had a 45-gallon drum of aviation fuel, so we filled both tanks. I checked everything over and prepared for the flight.

Bert and his wife brought the little girl to the plane and put her in the right seat. It was a bit difficult for them to fasten the seat belt around her frail body and the big blanket. We stood on the shore and prayed for the little girl and the flight to Red Lake.

We untied the rope and put it into the airplane. With the paddle, taken from the holder on the side of the floats, I pushed the plane out into the deeper water. I climbed in and

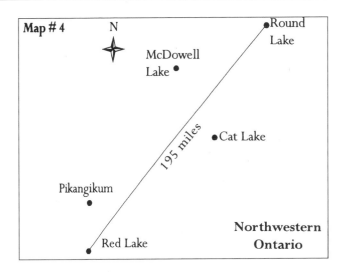

started the engine. The glistening of the moon on the lake prepared the "runway" for taking off. Once airborne, I could see the many lakes. With the flashlight I checked the map to follow the line across the lakes to Red Lake, 195 miles to the southwest.

I climbed to 4500 feet. I knew flying at night without lighted runways was not legal. But yet the glistening of the moon on the lakes did provide a "lighted" runway. Also, I could see many miles in every direction. One hour and thirty minutes later I landed at Red Lake on the golden "runway" made by the moonlight.

In the back of my mind I hoped the police would not be around, but sure enough, as I reached the dock, two police pulled up. I nervously tied the float to the dock wondering what would happen next. Deep in my heart I knew I had done the right thing.

After I finished tying the rope, I took a few extra seconds to accept whatever was to happen next. I stood up and said, "I have a very sick little girl here. Could you call a taxicab for me, please?" I carefully studied their facial expressions and body language.

With a compassionate voice one policeman answered, "No need for taxicab. In an emergency we will do what we can." They put the little girl into their cruiser. The knots in my stomach untied.

"Could I go along, too?" I asked.

"Sure," he repied.

They took the little girl and me to the emergency entrance and said, "If you need any more help, here's our number." To say the least, I was relieved.

Years later we met this girl in northern Manitoba. She was twenty-five. She thanked Clair for what he had done for her. Her father had often recounted this story to her to remind her of God's care.
— Clara

By now it was 1:15 a.m. I remained at the hospital to admit her on behalf of the Browns who had given me the medical report from the nurse back in Round Lake.

About 2 a.m. I found a place to sleep in Whitey's little cabin by the lake at Red Lake Seaplane Service.

The Browns kept in touch with the hospital via radio phone. The girl did recover and eventually returned to her family.

As I laid my head on the pillow that night, I knew that I had kept the spirit of the law. I was not bound by the letter of the law in this emergency situation when I knew a flight could be conducted safely within the spirit of the law.

Life Lesson   GOD KNOWS ALL ABOUT OUR INTENTIONS. HE IS ALSO CONCERNED THAT WE STUDY AND LEARN HIS LAWS. HE DOESN'T REQUIRE US TO BE RIGIDLY BOUND BY THE LETTER OF HIS LAWS, BUT HE WANTS US TO UNDERSTAND THE SPIRIT OF HIS COMMANDMENTS AND SINCERELY FOLLOW THEM.

• • •

One early spring day my wife and I were flying south to Pickle Lake in the small two-place Luscombe 8F from a community further north. We called ahead to tell Harvey Hochstetler to pick us up at the lake, because we were on skis.

As we approached Pickle Lake, I remembered that we had had a large amount of snow that winter and this was an early warm spring. I remembered my lesson well from the time at Red Lake when the airplane ended up on its nose. Pickle Lake is farther south than we had been flying. Deciding not to land on the deep, wet snow at the lake, I opted to land at the airport.

It is common procedure to land ski planes between the runway lights and the snow banks. The airport operators always keep the snow banks pushed well back from the runway lights. There is no pavement in that strip which left a nice area for landing ski planes.

I chose to land on the north side because that was where the terminal shack with fuel is located. The runway at Pickle Lake is in an east-west direction.

Before landing in an area like this, I like to make a low pass to check for any rocks and to see if there is enough snow for the skis. My left gas tank was full. I was using fuel from the right tank as I made a low pass at 500 feet. In order to see better, I lowered my left wing as I flew along the runway. To keep the plane going straight ahead, I had to push right rudder. Pilots call this cross controlling.

Three-quarters of the way down the runway, the engine quit. I straightened out the airplane and switched the fuel selector to the other tank, but that did not help. Engine failure at 500 feet did not give me much time to think or land.

I remembered the old adage, "Keep the nose down in a dead-stick landing. Keep up the glide speed until flaring out to land." I landed on the last ten to fifteen feet of the runway, but there was not enough runway remaining to stop.

In the few seconds I had to think, I remembered how the runway had been built. At the west end of the runway, there is a big dropoff because the hill goes down to the lake. All the tree stumps and big rocks were pushed down that hill.

As we went off the west end of the runway, I knew that we would hit rocks and tree stumps. I tried to say, "Clara, I'm sorry I am killing you." But I never finished the sentence.

There was nothing to do except to keep the airplane straight and level for the next few seconds and hit the tops of rocks and tree stumps.

"Oh Jesus, help us," Clara kept saying.

Those were a few scary seconds as we clipped the tops of the debris, taking off the skis first which slowed us down considerably before the final stop. The airplane ended up on its back. We were thankful there was no sudden stop! However, the airplane was seriously damaged.

My nose hit the aluminum dash, but not as hard as the time in 1962. It was bleeding heavily. I turned to my right side so I could help Clara loosen her seatbelt. She was

Hanging upside down in an airplane is an incredibly awesome experience. But I was more frightened when I was helpless to unbuckle my seatbelt. What a relief when Clair undid the belt, and in all my winter gear I rolled out the door onto the wing.
– Clara

hanging upside down. Her right knee had hit the bottom edge of the instrument panel and pushed the radios in an inch or two. Her knee was hurting and my nose was hurting, but otherwise we were all right. I had not killed my wife!

Clara crawled out and sat on the wing while I walked up the steep hill to the runway to find some help to move her to the nursing station. As I was walking down the runway, I met Dave Halteman coming to find us. He was a paramedic, so he called the ambulance to come for Clara because we did not know how badly her knee was injured.

The Pickle Lake nurse felt that we should go to the hospital for a full checkup, so she put us on the next plane to Thunder Bay. At the hospital, the doctor checked Clara's bruised knee and my broken nose. After some x-rays, we were released and someone was kind enough to take us to Dryden by car.

By the time we arrived home, Richard Newswanger had taken the wings off the airplane and hauled it to the hangar for repairs.

The next day Clara and I left for Arviat, Nunavut, to teach a seminar for youth. We used the twin-engine Piper Seneca II for that trip. We had an enjoyable time with the participants at the seminar. Also we had exceptionally good weather for the flights to Arviat and back to Dryden.

In time the Luscombe 8F was flying again. Upon investigation, it was confirmed that the cross controlling exercise had moved the gas by centrifugal force to the outside of the gas tank and away from the line to the engine. Also, the fuel selector was in the off position instead of the full tank position. But at five hundred feet and descending rapidly, it is doubtful that the gas from the full tank would have reached the engine in time to restart the engine before we hit the tree stumps and the rocks.

Life Lesson IF I LEARNED ANYTHING, IT WAS THE RE-ENFORCEMENT TO ALWAYS BE ON THE FULL TANK WHEN LANDING OR DOING LOW-LEVEL FLYING. THAT BECAME FIXED IN MY MIND AS STANDARD PROCEDURE. GOD WANTS US TO RUN ON "FULL TANKS." HE DELIGHTS IN FILLING OUR "TANKS" FROM HIS WORD AND BY PRAYER AND FELLOWSHIP WITH OTHERS.

•   •   •

One summer day I was doing some business at Slate Falls. When I was finished, my passenger and I taxied out for takeoff. Because of the direction of the wind, we had to taxi out some extra distance to where I had never been before.

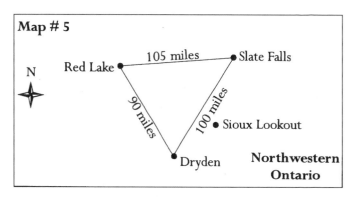

All of a sudden one float became stuck on a rock a few inches under the water. We could not move off the spot, because we were hung up on the rock.

Back at the dock, some men saw our predicament. They came out with a boat and pulled the airplane off the rock. Then I could hear water gushing into the largest compartment in the center of the right float.

I grabbed a rope and threw one end to the men in the boat. The other end I threw to my passenger who was standing on the front of the right float. He held the rope as the boat was moving into position to tow us.

I yelled above the noise, "Pull us to the closest shore."

They gave that twenty-five-horsepower boat motor full throttle. I knew that as long as we kept moving, the water would not gush into the float but would slide past the hole in the bottom of the float.

My passenger, a strong man, used every bit of energy to hang onto that rope. His knuckles turned white, but he and I knew that if he would let go of the rope, the airplane would go underwater very quickly. Also, I used the hand pump to get rid of the water that had already gushed into the float. My passenger held that rope tightly as the men in the boat pulled us to shore.

As they reached the rock shore, the men jumped out of the boat and pulled us onto a big flat rock.

Hearing the passenger's side of the story was very interesting. The adrenaline rush gave him the strength to hang on.

– Clara

By this time that float was underwater but firmly on the rock. Then we pulled the front part of the float out of the water as far as possible. With the hand pump we pumped out as much water as we could. Then we pulled the airplane up higher on the rocks and pumped again. At last the large compartment that had the hole in it was up on the flat rock. We didn't need to pump anymore because the water ran out the hole.

After the airplane was out of the water, the men found two logs. As we lifted the airplane, they pushed the two logs under the float so we could assess the size and type of hole the rock had made. We decided that we could make a temporary repair. The men went back to the village and were able to find what was needed to make a temporary repair with a piece of sheet metal, screws and pitch.

Fortunately another airplane came in from Red Lake and took my passenger to Red Lake while I flew the Luscombe 8F to Red Lake Seaplane Service. The mechanics did a proper repair with aluminum and rivets.

After the repair work, we had an uneventful flight back to Dryden. We cancelled the rest of that trip, because there were other schedules to keep back home.

Life Lesson   AT TIMES IN OUR LIVES THE
BURDENS AND PRESSURES OF
LIFE BECOME HEAVY. WE FEEL AS IF WE ARE GOING UNDER,
BUT AS WE PRAY AND TALK WITH A FRIEND, WE KNOW GOD
IS THERE TO STRENGTHEN AND HELP US HANDLE THOSE
TIMES IN OUR LIVES WHEN WE FEEL AS IF WE ARE GOING
UNDER. HE CARES.

•   •   •

One very cold windy January afternoon Clara and I and
several Inuit friends landed on the airstrip at Kaktovik (Barter
Island), Alaska. We had planned for three evenings of teaching
and music. After unloading the airplane, we loaded our gear
into the van that our friend George had brought out to take us
into town.

When I saw Clair on the snow-covered ground, his face was ashen. But DENIAL works for a while! Women sometimes have to watch their men suffer until they come out of denial.
– Clara

Before we left for town, we
needed to put covers on the wings.
While I was up on the right wing,
somehow I slipped off, falling on
my left leg. It really hurt! When
I went to the nursing station to
have it checked, the nurse thought
it was broken, but I felt like it was
only a sprained ankle. Two days
later the leg began to swell and
hurt severely.

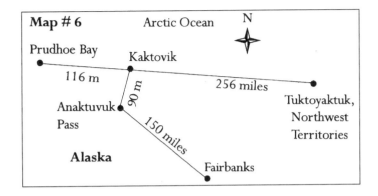

Early one morning, before people were stirring, I crawled to the nursing station, because I was too ashamed to ask for help. I agreed with the nurse that my leg was broken. A call was made for an airplane to come in to fly me out to the Fairbanks hospital.

On that flight I was not the pilot; I was the patient. This was a role reversal and I must admit, humiliating. I was especially embarrassed for slipping off the wing. This was a good experience for me to be the weak one needing help.

I was back in the community. I was glad Clair went to the hospital. I slept well when he was gone knowing he was where he could obtain help.

– Clara

The surgeon did his work well. Today I still have a plate and five screws in my left leg. Thanks to the excellent surgeon and the people who prayed that my leg would heal properly, it did. Today I walk without a limp.

After I returned from the hospital, we finished the trip with chartered airplanes. Yes, it was more expensive, but we completed the seminars. The people in each community gave me much help to move around with my crutches in the deep snow. Later I went back for my own airplane.

Life Lesson   GOD IS ALWAYS GOD OF OUR LIVES AND HEARTS. EMERGENCIES NEVER CATCH GOD OFF GUARD. HE KNOWS ALL ABOUT HOW TO HELP IN WHATEVER WAY HE CAN.

5

MY DAUGHTERS AND WIFE LEARN TO FLY

J udy splashed into the water. The flight examiner from Winnipeg, Manitoba, was watching seventeen-year-old Judy do her preflight check before the flight test. Proper preparation is an important part of flying.

Funny, Judy.
– Cathie

Judy had been standing on the float of the Luscombe 8F to check the oil before the flight. This was a normal procedure. Nonetheless, she was nervous, as all student pilots are before the flight test ride with the Ministry of Transport (MOT) flight examiner. Her one foot slipped and she fell into the water. She was totally immersed. Being a good swimmer, she swam to the dock and climbed out.

As she stood up, dripping wet, Judy finally had the nerve to look the flight inspector in the eyes.

He was smiling and said, "Well, every bush pilot needs to fall into the water at least once."

*I had
taken Judy
by car to
the airplane,
because she
still did not
have her
driver's license.
I will never
forget the little
shriek and
the splash. I
knew what had
happened!
– Clara*

His gentle reply and manner were reassuring to Judy. She could feel her confidence level rise again. His kind manner put her more at ease about the upcoming private pilot's test flight on floats.

Clara drove Judy to a friend's house where she changed clothing and came back to finish her preflight checks. She did the flight test ride and passed. The examiner was quite pleased with her flying abilities. She was a private pilot on floats! Later she had to be checked out for skis and wheels.

The next week she took her driver's test ride and failed! She redeemed herself by trying again the following week when she did pass her driver's test.

Several of my daughters had spent hours flying with me for the purpose of building father-daughter relationships. They would take turns sitting in the right seat, while I sat in the left seat. One winter several of them needed flight training with a licensed instructor. That winter, Ian Pentney, a water bomber pilot for the Ministry of Natural Resources, had nothing special to do. He was a certified flight instructor and offered as much time as was needed for a nominal fee.

With small pine trees we marked out an east-west landing area (a "runway" for skis) on the lake in front of our house. For a period of several months, our house resembled a flight school. Flying was the main topic at every meal.

At the beginning of that time, my wife asked to talk with me privately. She began the conversation by saying, "Clair, you know about my fear of flying. I do fly with you as part of the Youth and Family Seminar Ministry, but I am afraid of flying. There is still a lot of fear of the unknown. I have asked God to give me a promise that would help me with my fear, but now I sense that He is asking me to do the impossible and learn to fly so He can help me with my fear! Do you think my fears would be relieved if I took flying lessons and understood the dynamics of airplanes? Often I don't know what is normal and what is abnormal. That creates fear within me. What do you think?"

God had given me many promises to take away my fears in different circumstances. It amazed me that God chose this route to overcome my fear. I was a woman of 42 at the time. Today I am thankful He chose that path for me. Now I enjoy assisting Clair in all our flights.

– Clara

I was stunned. Was I dreaming? My wife, talking about flying lessons, was completely beyond my wildest imaginations. "Why . . . why . . . yeah! Of course flying lessons would help you overcome your fears," I finally replied.

"Okay, I am ready to start tomorrow," was her reply.

"I'll plan with Ian tonight and we will schedule you for tomorrow," I said.

The next day was the beginning of thirty-five hours of lessons for Clara that winter. In between the flying lessons she studied for the written exam, took the exam and passed with a higher score than I had twenty-five years before.

One day Clara said, "I am having a lot of trouble with the final flareout for the landings. Will you fly with me first thing in the morning and give me any additional pointers?"

"Sure," I said. "Look, all you need to do is break the glide speed by pulling the throttle some and fly straight and level just above the ground. Just keep pulling back the throttle and applying a little back pressure on the yoke. It will nicely settle on the ground. Then cut the throttle completely and, with the rudders, steer to a stop. Then you have landed."

"Oh, you mean that's all it takes?" she asked quizzically.

"Yes, that's all," were my words as I gave her a smile.

"All right, first thing in the morning, I'll do just that," she said.

First thing in the morning Clara and I did some circuits. She did well on takeoff, climbout and level flight. Her radio work was excellent. I was amazed at her proficiency. She trimmed the airplane perfectly for level flight. She set up an excellent glide speed for landing. She flared out about ten feet above the ground and pulled back slightly on the throttle to reduce the speed. She flew straight and level right down the runway. Slowly she reduced the power and applied back pressure on the yoke. She made a very smooth landing.

She exclaimed, "I got it. Is it really that easy or was it just an accident?"

"Yes, Clara," I said, "it is that easy."

"My instructor will be very pleased!" she replied.

Her scheduled flight with the instructor was twice as long the next day. He was surprised at her ability to land the airplane properly, so they did takeoffs and landings for almost an hour, first on the "runway" and then on other unmarked places on the lake and on other lakes too.

On one of these landings, he said, "You must remember when you are flying by yourself that the plane is lighter and will glide a little farther."

That made sense to her. When she landed, to her surprise, the instructor opened his door and climbed out. He said, "Just do as you have been doing. Just remember the glide will be a little longer." He closed the door and walked away.

Clara mechanically taxied back to the beginning of the trees in the snow that marked the "runway." She did an excellent takeoff. In the circuit she finally realized that she was all alone in the airplane. Her knees began to knock. *Clara, relax and just do as you have always done*, she said to herself. She came around and did a perfect landing. The airplane came to a halt across from where the instructor was still standing.

Clara had accomplished a solo flight successfully! Her instructor walked over and said, "Good job, Mrs. Schnupp. You're becoming a pro. Do you want to make another circuit by yourself?" he asked.

"No, I want to go and tell my husband I did it," she said.

So, bouncing into the house came a happy instructor and an excited lady. She exclaimed to me, "Do you have time to go along for a ride with me?"

"Sure, let's go," was my elated response.

Away we went. I was amazed at Clara's ability to do pre-flight checks, the run-up, taxiing, radio work, takeoff, climbout and trimming out for level flight. Her glide was excellent and the flareout was perfect. The landing was superb.

"You did it, babe! I'm proud of you!" I said. She smiled and was as proud as a peacock.

The instructor continued teaching the girls. I went off to the office. Whatever I had said to Clara that morning before "clicked." What the instructor thought is still a mystery to me.

The next morning she told the instructor and me that her fear of flying was gone. "I am finished training now. I trained and studied, not to fly, but to deal with my fears. I accomplished what I wanted." That was her first and last solo flight.

•   •   •

Sharon, my second daughter, finished her pilot's training and acquired her private pilot's licence.

In addition to her flying, music, teacher's training in university, crushes on good guys, youth group activities, and sewing, she became a salesperson for Successful Living Books.

She wanted to do a fly-in book trip with her friend, Rhoda Herschberger, to several communities where she knew many people. They wanted to sell good books. They set the date and selected and packed the books. They weighed every box carefully. After loading the airplane, Sharon did all the preflight checks and away they flew in the float plane.

On that trip they had good weather and light winds. They enjoyed the people and sold some very good books as they stood behind two tables and a big sign reading, "Good Books For Sale." The profit was not enough to pay for the fuel. We, as Sharon's parents, paid for the fuel, because this trip was providing good bush flying experience for her. The trip also provided meaningful interaction with the people for both Sharon and Rhoda.

There were skeptics about girls being bush pilots. But Sharon and Rhoda knew how to survive in the bush, because they grew up in that country and were part of many family campouts and canoe trips.

By 1975 we purchased a Cessna 206 and travelled as a family to conduct Family Life Seminars in Canada, Alaska, Mexico and Central America. On each trip we would take along as many of the daughters who could adjust their schedules to the travel plans.

Flying with the Cessna 206 meant that we could go more places, which required more hours in the sky. I knew that father-daughter (and father-son) relationships were important for proper and healthy child development into adulthood. As soon as the girls could see over the dash, I would have them take turns sitting in the right seat beside me. All of our airplanes have dual controls. My enthusiasm for flying rubbed off

Clair was teaching dads to be involved with their children. He wanted to do more things with his own daughters. The Holy Spirit was at work in his heart too.

– Clara

onto my daughters. I taught them about the instruments and what the controls do. Then they would practice straight and level flying. Slowly they advanced until they could take off, climb out, fly and navigate. There was no GPS (Global Positioning System) in those days; the flying was done by maps and visual landmarks.

As we flew together there were times when we could talk about life issues through the headsets. We always made sure the radio mikes were off! We kept monitoring the appropriate frequencies for other air traffic or airport radio operators that might be close by.

Those times were important to me. Now my daughters have families of their own, but precious memories will remain forever!

Life Lesson THOSE HOURS OF TOGETHERNESS WHILE FLYING AND DIALOGUING HELPED BUILD AND MAINTAIN HEALTHY FATHER-DAUGHTER RELATIONSHIPS WITH A UNIQUE PURPOSE.

•   •   •

"Come teach the Family Life Seminar at our tent meetings and in our churches," requested Alex Beardy from Big Trout Lake, Ontario. Alex was a respected, godly leader throughout northwestern Ontario.

Our family decided to do what we could to fulfill Alex Beardy's requests. Sharon and Carolyn would fly the Luscombe

8F on floats while Judy and I would fly the Cessna 206 on floats. Our family and Alex would number eight: two in the Luscombe 8F and six in the Cessna 206. The communities were not far apart and we kept the overnight bags small.

> This was a major time when I had to learn to trust Clair's decisions. It was not easy. But he really believed in his girls.
>
> – Clara

During those trips the two planes always travelled together. We kept in contact with each other via radio. Things had changed between 1962 and 1980. By 1980, the airplanes had batteries, generators, starters, good compasses and radios. The airplanes I flew in 1962 had none of those.

As on all our longer trips, the twenty gallons of gas for the Luscombe 8F was not quite enough. Sharon and Carolyn took a five-gallon can of aviation gas along. At about the half-way point they landed on a lake while Judy and I circled overhead until they had the five gallons of gas poured into the wing tank as the airplane slowly bobbed up and down on the waves. Carolyn was usually up on the wing and Sharon was on the float during the refueling process. Filling airplanes with fuel was as familiar to them as brushing their

> Amazing.
> – Mary

teeth. In a few minutes they would be airborne again, and we would continue on our way. We usually flew at a good altitude to follow the maps and the lakes and rivers.

One time Alex wanted to make a trip from Big Trout Lake, Ontario, to Fort Severn on the Hudson Bay coast and to Bearskin Lake. Alex had made all the arrangements ahead of time for the lodging, meals and places for the seminars. We had many good times with the families who looked after us and there was always more food than we could eat. None of us could afford to gain much weight on those trips; the planes would not handle it!

Sharon and Carolyn would always take off first. The Luscombe 8F was slower than the Cessna 206, which meant that Sharon and Carolyn needed a head start. Then Judy and I would take off and arrive at the destination first to give them any assistance they might need to tie the airplanes in a safe place. The planes needed to be tied well with long ropes in case of any storms during the night.

Sharon was Alex's favourite pilot, because she would always make perfect takeoffs and landings—at least in his perception. He nicknamed her "Sky Bird." He would say, "Sky Bird can do it. She loves the skies like the birds."

At Fort Severn on that trip, we were loading the airplanes for departure as well as doing the preflight checks and pumping any water out of the floats that may have seeped in during our stay. A float has hundreds of rivets and most floats will develop a slow leak here or there.

Both airplanes were parked close together for refueling and loading. During the refueling process, Judy shouted, "The keys have just fallen into the muddy Severn River!"

Unfortunately we did not carry a second set of keys. Not only was the Severn River muddy, but the current moved along with some strength toward the mighty Hudson Bay. We were in trouble.

"We need those keys. I realize it was an accident, but we still need those keys," I exclaimed.

Judy was an excellent swimmer and loved water like a fish. She mentally calculated the possible depth of the water and the speed of the current. Then she dove down into the muddy river, fully clothed. When she surfaced she had the keys between her teeth. What a miracle that was!

Life Lesson *I LEARNED SEVERAL LESSONS FROM THAT EXPERIENCE. WITH FLOAT PLANES WE NOW HAVE A FLOTATION DEVICE ON THE KEY CHAIN AS WELL AS A SPARE KEY SCREWED TO THE AIRPLANE IN AN INCONSPICUOUS PLACE.*

Finally we were ready to fly to Bearskin Lake. Sharon and Carolyn taxied out and took off first. After they were airborne and on their way, Judy and I taxied out, took off and climbed to an altitude of 6500 feet, bound for Bearskin Lake, Ontario.

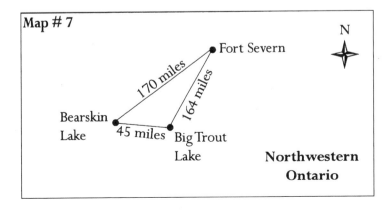

After landing and securing the airplanes, we went to our places of lodging. The Family Life Seminar was good. The girls, as usual, spent meaningful time with the children. These children enjoyed stories, puppets and songs while Clara and I conducted the seminars with the adults.

Several days later we were preparing to go to another community when, suddenly, Judy shouted, "My wallet fell into the water!" At Bearskin Lake the water was still and not muddy. Just as quickly as her wallet fell into the lake, Judy dove down and surfaced with the wallet between her teeth.

Sharon was Alex's "Sky Bird" and Judy was his "Water Bird."

We had many good times on those trips.

•   •   •

It was winter time. We were using the Cessna 206 equipped with hydraulic wheel-skis. After finishing a Youth Seminar at Keewaytin Bible Institute, Lac La Biche, Alberta, we planned to travel to Montreal Lakes, Saskatchewan, for another Youth Seminar at Montreal Lakes Children's Home.

As Clara and I finished up the seminar, Sharon, who was the pilot-in-command, called the Aviation Weather Services for weather and to file the flight plan. As she was finishing the preflight checks, we arrived, loaded our gear and boarded the plane. Sharon was in the pilot's seat and Carolyn was in the co-pilot's seat. Clara and I were in the middle seats because we had some things to talk about on that trip. Cathie and Mary were in the back seats.

Sharon had all the maps folded and in proper order. As we were taxiing out, I leaned forward and asked her what the weather was like enroute and at the destination.

"Good, with a thirty percent chance of snow in the area of our destination," she said.

"Sounds good enough to me. At least we have skis if the snow gets too heavy and we need to land on a lake," I replied.

Sharon did all the radio work, taxied out and away we went at 5500 feet for Montreal Lakes, two hours away. We had four hours and thirty minutes of fuel. All seemed good to me. After Clara and I had our talk, I had a good nap. I was awakened by Sharon's nervous words, "Dad, it's snowing and we are down to 2500 feet. Do you think we should prepare to land?"

I rubbed my eyes, evaluated the situation and said, "If you were here without me, I would certainly say find a place to land and set up camp. But I am along. Carolyn and I will exchange seats. Together you and I will see if we can make Montreal Lakes."

Carolyn and I exchanged seats. I can fly right or left seat just as well. Either seat makes no difference to me.

"Sharon, can you show me on the map exactly where we are? Which lake is this one?" I asked.

Pointing to a lake marked on the map, Sharon replied, "We are here, and this lake is just ahead of us."

She was right on course and heading the correct direction. "How far is it to Montreal Lakes?" I asked.

"Oh, about thirty-five nautical miles and approximately twenty minutes," was her response.

At that time, the snow was becoming thicker and visibility was three to five miles. We were approximately 1500 feet above the trees and lakes.

This still makes me smile.
– Sharon

"Sharon, can you let me be the pilot-in-command?" I asked.

"Yes, certainly. It's all yours, Dad. I would already be landed by a shore someplace and be setting up camp for the night," Sharon responded.

"I agree," I said and continued. "You make good judgments. That's what makes you a good and safe pilot. I trust you."

At that time, I had about 7000 hours of bush flying in all kinds of weather. I knew my limits and had camped out overnight more than once.

We were too low to reach anyone on the radio to ask for more weather information ahead. I had the map and was carefully keeping the straight line over the lakes and trees. The snow was becoming thicker and the visibility was about three miles. I had descended to 1000 feet above the trees. We were ten miles from our destination and it seemed that we should be able to arrive safely. Just then I noticed that we had flown over a cabin that looked quite well-kept. There was no path to a water hole and no smoke coming out of the chimney. That told me that no one was living there at the time. By this time, the snow was falling more heavily, the visibility was much less than three miles and we were at 600 feet. The thought rushed through my mind, *Those who* ***must*** *make the destination at all costs often pay for it with their lives.*

> I was peering out the window, drifting between sleep and fear.
> – Cathie

No second thoughts. I made a 180-degree turn back to the cabin and landed straight ahead on the snow-covered lake by the cabin. The temperature was -25°F.

We were all thankful to be down safely and close to a cabin. I turned the plane around and taxied back towards the cabin. All was well, I thought. We would soon be in the cabin with a roaring, crackling fire enjoying a good evening of relaxation. Unfortunately I was not watching for slush as I should have been.

Suddenly, I noticed that the snow closer to the shore was not drifted and seemed deep and fluffy. I was prepared to stop and walk the one hundred yards to the shore to check for slush and to look around at the cabin. But then I had that sinking feeling and saw the slush flying from my left ski. I pushed full power to keep moving back to the solid snow, but the slush was too deep and the Cessna 206 came to a sudden stop. The skis were on solid ice that was about three feet thick. They were in about ten inches of water and slush. We were stuck.

"We are in big trouble," I said.

Everyone was quiet. They all knew what slush meant.

"I'll get out and check the cabin and check how far the slush goes," I said.

The slush was almost to the shore and the cabin seemed to be in good condition. There was a pile of stove wood against the cabin by the door and we all knew that cabins in remote areas are seldom locked so they can be used by stranded travellers.

I made my way back to the airplane. I told my family about the cabin but that first we had to move the airplane out of the slush before it froze fast.

The plan was for Clara and the youngest girls to sit in the back seats so the nose ski would have less weight on it. It would ride higher to make it easier for the airplane to move out onto the solid snow before the skis froze in the slush.

The others were to help me tramp the snow into the water between the snow and the ice. Hopefully we could make a path that would allow the airplane motor to pull the airplane through the slush onto solid snow. But this meant that we three would have wet feet and would need to rush to the cabin as soon as possible once the airplane was out of the slush.

We climbed out and began to tramp snow into the water. After we had about twelve feet tramped down ahead of each ski,

We laughed, sang and almost cried at times as we worked together.
— Sharon

I climbed into the airplane and started the motor. With Sharon pushing on one wing strut and Carolyn pushing on the other wing strut, I gave the engine full power. The plane moved only a few inches.

At one point, Carolyn said, "I think our tramped path is sticky with too much water. Why don't we push more loose snow into the slush to make it thicker and harder? This would act like a ramp from the lower level to the higher level. In this way, maybe the skis will slide better." We all agreed.

By this time, we had not called back to Lac La Biche because we had no way of letting them know where we were. We could not cancel the flight plan, so Flight Services would report us missing to our home base in Dryden, Ontario. Montreal Lakes knew we were not there either. That Wednesday night three prayer groups were praying for us—Lac La Biche, Montreal Lakes and Dryden. I believe Carolyn's wise idea came because of the prayer meetings.

With the reality that darkness was fast coming upon us, we tried Carolyn's new idea, in spite of Sharon complaining about cold feet. I showed concern by saying, "Sharon, my feet are cold too, but as long as our feet are in the water they will not freeze. Let's finish Carolyn's plan and then we can get to the cabin fast and start a roaring fire."

> *I sure was! And believe me, there was good reason to complain, thank you!*
> *– Sharon*

Finally we had a path filled with loose snow which we carried in, kicked in and pushed in. The slush did thicken more and eventually seemed more solid and less sticky.

We decided that I should try again to move the airplane forward. Clara and the youngest girls were still in the back seats to help reduce the weight on the nose ski. Then with one girl ready to push on the left strut and another girl ready to push on the right one, I climbed into the airplane and started the engine. I pushed full throttle, the girls pushed on the wing struts with all their might, and the airplane slowly moved until we were out onto the solid snow!

Then there was a mad rush to the cabin. As quickly as possible, we started a fire to keep our feet from freezing. We were thankful for the barrel stove and the good wood. Soon the fire was roaring and the heat filled the cabin. We were able to find some dry clothes in the drawers, so we hung up our wet clothing to dry during the night.

It was a beautiful, relaxed, cozy feeling to be warm, have hot food and know we could fly out of there the next day.
– Clara

Clara found some food and black tea in the cupboard. She even found a large can of chicken and soon had some food ready to eat. Of course, anything would have tasted good that night. We enjoyed the food and the hot tea as we warmed our bodies by the red hot stove.

Eventually we found enough dry clothing for Sharon and me to trek out to the airplane to get the sleeping bags. While we were out there we started the Coleman catalytic heater and put it under the engine cowling to keep the engine warm during the night. We also covered the engine with the quilted cover.

Finally we were all in the cabin for the night—warm, happy and tired. We rolled out our sleeping bags with some on the bed and the others on the floor. The bags were good, down-filled sleeping bags tested at -40°F. At least that is what the tag said. Snuggling into our sleeping bags, we talked and laughed some more. We were on an adventure out in the wild. Together, we had just conquered the almost unconquerable, and everyone was safe and warm.

By dawn we were up. Clara prepared some rolled oats and black tea for breakfast while the rest of us tidied up the cabin, trying to leave it as we found it. We also put some money in a cup in the cupboard. We found the address of the owners on an old envelope. Later that day we sent them a letter of appreciation and told them where we had left the money.

By the time we were loaded and had the motor running to take off, there was a Search and Rescue Beaver ski plane flying overhead. We were able to talk together on the radios and I assured them that we were fine. I explained that we had flown into heavy snow and slept in the cabin.

They told us that they would circle overhead until we were airborne and on our way to Montreal Lakes. After we were airborne I thanked them for the good services of Search and Rescue.

Yes, we were all fine, except for little Mary. The night before, she had stayed in the airplane with Clara, so she did not have wet feet when we were getting the plane unstuck. However, the next morning, while walking across the snow-covered ice from the cabin to the airplane, Mary's one foot went down into the slush. Her boot became soaked with water and she had a very cold foot. Clara had a crying little girl to care for during the ten-minute flight to Montreal Lakes.

When we arrived at Montreal Lakes, Clara took care of Mary's cold, wet foot while I phoned Lac La Biche and Dryden. All were glad to hear that we were safe.

We had a good seminar at Montreal Lakes. A few days later we were back in Dryden. It was good to be home.

Later, the couple who owned the cabin answered our letter, explaining that we did not have to leave any money. They explained what I often heard: "During emergencies in the bush country, anybody's cabin and its contents are to be used for survival." We appreciated their note.

Life Lesson WITH CONCENTRATED EFFORT AND PRAYER, MANY DIFFICULT TASKS CAN BE ACCOMPLISHED IN LIFE. WE NEED EACH OTHER AND GOD.

•   •   •

One winter night we finished a Family Seminar in a small community. Lodging was not easy to find so we agreed to sleep in the church. Some of the girls put their sleeping bags on the benches, others, on the floor.

Clara and the girls were already in their sleeping bags by the time I went to plug in the airplane. By that time we had an electric heater on the engine. We had landed on the frozen lake by the village and tried to park close enough to the church for our 100-foot electric cord.

When I rolled out the electric cord, I lacked twelve inches. I had no idea where to find more cord, so I went back to the church where the girls were in their sleeping bags. We had been there so long that the engine in the Cessna 206 was too cold to start. The outside temperature was about -29°F.

I needed help to push the airplane forward one foot. I went into the church and said, "I have a serious problem. I need help. The cow is having a calf. The calf is stuck sideways and I cannot pull it out."

> Thank you, Dad, for teaching us to work and to work with you.
> – Sharon

As you can tell, I was a farm boy and I did not want my daughters to think that only families who sing and teach Youth and Family Seminars have problems that require off-duty time. They all understood the point. A big groan arose in unison.

"I cannot do it by myself," I said. "We can just let it go for tonight and do it in the morning, but we would have to wait until noon to leave for home." Another groan arose.

"It is your choice," I said.

Then one by one they crawled out of their sleeping bags. They put on their parkas, big boots and mittens. It didn't take us more than two minutes to "help the cow have a calf" and move the plane forward one foot.

> Oh, for the good old days!
> – Sharon

Everyone crawled back into their sleeping bags for a good night of sleep. Shortly after sunrise we were on our way home with Sharon as pilot-in-command. It was an uneventful flight home. When we arrived, I told Sharon, "You did a good job."

"Thank you," she replied.

• • •

One summer Judy was flying gas from Red Lake into Poplar Hill to add to one of my many gas caches in Northwestern Ontario. I was at the Red Lake Seaplane base helping the mechanics do some work on the Cessna 206.

Darkness set in and Judy was not back. She was one hour overdue. I had not heard from her and it was getting late. The lake was calm and any landing would be a glassy water landing. Where could she be?

Clair called me from Red Lake. "Judy is not back and we have not heard from her." Deep, paralyzing fear gripped me.
— Clara

I called Poplar Hill and Pikangikum. I found out that on her route to Poplar Hill, Judy had changed her destination to Pikangikum because the lakes were becoming calm. I also found out that she had left the gas cache at Pikangikum and headed back to Red Lake. So

Life Lesson IT DOESN'T MATTER HOW HARD ONE WORKS FOR GOD OR HOW MUCH ONE SACRIFICES TO WORK FOR GOD. THERE IS NO GUARANTEE THAT ALL WILL GO WELL. MY GRANDPA ALWAYS SAID, "CLAIR, THE RAIN FALLS ON THE JUST AND THE UNJUST."

she was not at Pikangikum and had not arrived back in Red Lake.

I chartered a Piper Aztec to take me on a night flight to see if there was any sign of any unusual campfire. The pilot and I flew low over Stormer Lake which had no telephone. The best we could see in the moonlight, there was no small red and white airplane tied up at their dock.

Dad would do anything, spend any amount of money or move anywhere if it would help his daughters.
— Carolyn

I and other concerned friends decided to meet at 7 a.m. if Judy didn't return soon after sunrise. We would make grids over the possible areas where Judy could be and decide who would fly over the various grids in search of the little red and white Luscombe 8F and Judy.

At 2 a.m., a medivac plane took off from Red Lake for Sandy Lake. Thunder Bay radio asked them to be on the lookout for any sign of a small plane that had not returned to Red Lake the previous evening.

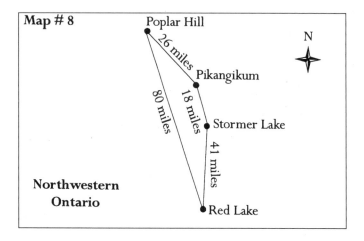

The medivac pilot asked, "Is it Luscombe C-FYCG?"

"That's correct," Thunder Bay radio said.

The pilot told Thunder Bay radio that when he was landing the previous evening, he heard C-FYCG give a message to another pilot to phone her dad at 727-3610. He was to inform her dad that because it was late and the lakes were smooth and glassy, she was landing at Stormer Lake for the night. She would come to Red Lake first thing in the morning.

Thunder Bay Flight Service called Red Lake at 2:15 a.m. to relay Judy's message. It was a relief to receive that good news. I had never received any call nor had anyone else at Red Lake Seaplane Service the evening before. Some pilot had been distracted with other matters and never called us. I went to a little cabin Red Lake and had a good sleep.

In the morning, after Judy returned, I took her out for breakfast. We chatted about the events of the day before. I assured her that she had done the right thing by not continuing to fly in conditions beyond what she felt she could safely handle. We discussed how safety always comes first and that pilots with "get-home-itis" often do not live long. We talked about the old saying: "There are old pilots and there are bold pilots, but there are no old, bold pilots." Over-confidence has killed more than one pilot.

Life Lesson I LEARNED FROM THIS EXPERIENCE TO BE CAREFUL TO COMMUNICATE WHAT WE WANT TO COMMUNICATE TO THE RIGHT PEOPLE. WHENEVER THERE IS A BREAK IN ONE LINK OF THE COMMUNICATION CHAIN, SOMETHING WILL GO WRONG OR SOMEONE WILL GET HURT OR SOME RELATIONSHIP MAY BE WOUNDED.

6

MOUNTAIN FLYING

“Some clouds have granite centres,” is a phrase used when talking about flying in mountainous regions. What may appear as a soft, fluffy cloud can hide a hard, unforgiving mountain peak. A pilot flying in mountainous areas in wintertime must exercise much caution.

When flying by visual flight rules (VFR), a pilot is to stay away from clouds. But when flying through mountain passes, things can become tricky very quickly. This is especially true when almost everything is snow-covered on a gray, cloud-covered day. A VFR pilot can easily lose any sense of orientation and fly into a snow-covered hill or mountain.

Before I flew in any new or different types of geographical areas—in mountainous places or in the Arctic regions—I always talked with experienced pilots and read books about those areas. I wanted to know the advantages and disadvantages. Also, I wanted to learn how to fly and survive. Each type of geographical area presents its unique challenges to a pilot.

Once we had booked seminars in mountainous communities and beyond, I bought a book on mountain flying. I also talked with a friend, Dwayne King, who was a pilot with many hours of flying to and from Alaska. He had also done much flying in Alaska since he was based in Glenallen, Alaska.

I learned how to use mountain air currents to the pilot's advantage. The book also outlined the dangers of flying through mountain passes. It said that many mountain passes have a few demolished aircraft hanging on the mountainsides. Most of those pilots and passengers lost their lives.

The reason for using mountain passes is because most small planes are not supplied with oxygen tanks and masks. Ten to twelve thousand feet is considered the maximum altitude for any given flight without supplementary oxygen.

Dwayne spoke of missing the pass entrance and flying into a box canyon with no way out and too narrow to turn around. It can easily be a fatal mistake.

The book spoke of becoming caught in sudden storm squalls. If it is winter and the ground and mountains are covered with snow, a VFR pilot can easily find him/herself in a whiteout condition. In a whiteout condition a VFR pilot can easily lose all sense of orientation. The result is a downward left or right spiral into the ground or mountainside. There was much emphasis on how VFR pilots can avoid being caught in box canyons and whiteout conditions.

With that information I have safely flown in mountainous regions with members of my family.

On the flip side is all the grandeur, awe and beauty of flying in the mountainous regions and through mountain passes. Some of the mountains are very high. Mount McKinley is awesome, rugged and beautiful at 20,320 feet.

One summer we taught a Family Life Seminar in Carmacks, Yukon Territory. We were in the Cessna 206 on wheels. We had finished the Seminar about 9 p.m. and were to fly to Glennallen, Alaska, the next day.

I phoned the Aviation Weather Services and was informed that a bad weather front was moving in from the northwest and would reach the area about 2 a.m. Clara, the girls and I discussed the situation. We were also told that it was daylight until 12:15 a.m. We decided to quickly pack our belongings, load the plane, do the preflight checks and depart as soon as possible.

We were airborne by 10 p.m. for Northway, Alaska, where we planned to do customs and sleep in the motel. That way we would be over halfway to Glenallen and would have flown through the mountain pass before the bad weather came in from the northwest.

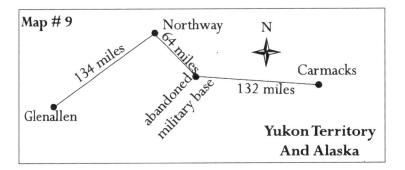

Sharon was the pilot-in-command. The pass went west and then northwest. The flight was to take one hour and twenty minutes. As we were flying through the mountain pass, we flew over an abandoned military base. The buildings looked dilapidated and the runway had been gravel, but since the war, grass had grown. I noticed many gopher holes on the old runway. I looked at the airstrip very carefully just in case we would need to turn back, because there would not be enough daylight to fly all the way back to Carmacks.

It was awesome, breathtaking scenery.
– Clara

We droned through the pass at about 3500 feet above the floor of the pass. Where the old military base was located, there was a nice valley for approaches to either runway. When we flew over I noticed a frequently used dirt bike trail right down the middle of the old runway. When we were 25 minutes from Northway, Alaska, we saw the fog and mist ahead. It was right down to the floor of the pass.

Oh, no, I thought, *the bad weather front had moved in faster than expected.*

My daughter looked at me and said, "Dad, that fog and mist seem to go right down to the trees. I think our only option is to go back to the abandoned military base before darkness sets in completely."

"A very wise decision for a pilot to make when there are really no other options," I agreed.

"Dad, do you think the gravel strip at the abandoned military base is good enough to land on?" she asked.

"Yes. The grass has grown and there are gopher holes. But there is a well-used dirt bike trail right down the center of that old runway. When you land, why not try to keep the nose wheel on that dirt bike trail? I looked carefully when we flew over the strip. There were no gopher holes on that dirt bike trail. We don't want to have the nose wheel drop into a gopher hole, because it would break off and we would end up on the nose, which would be very serious. The main gear is much stronger and more flexible, as you know. The main gear will be able to handle the gopher holes," I told her.

"I get it, Dad, and it looks like the old military base between the mountains is just coming into sight. I will land from west to east. I'll keep that nose wheel right on the dirt bike trail," she explained.

"Good girl, I know you can do it," I said. I watched as she did a perfect landing and taxied up to what must have been the old tower and terminal building. Everything looked so forsaken and drab.

We scouted around to find a room where we could all eat and sleep. Most of the windows were broken, and more discouraging, rain had begun and was dripping through the roofs and ceilings.

Clara said, "We should find a room for our sleeping bags and maybe make some black tea on the Coleman stove we have along. The heat will also keep us from getting too chilled."

"I can't agree with you more. Some of us will unload what we need tonight. We will keep things under the wing so they don't get wet from this rain. Why don't you take another good

look at the buildings? There must be one room that is dry," I suggested.

Within minutes Clara was back. "We found one room about twenty feet square that has no broken windows. The room has two stories above it, so there is no rain dripping into that room. It is just perfect for tonight," she exclaimed. "We'll set up the Coleman stove and set some cans where water is dripping off the roof to collect water for tea and cooking. We will make some black tea while the rest of you carry the sleeping bags and night bags into the building."

Interesting. Such neat memories. — Carolyn

My practical wife was excited about the one small, dry room without a rotten floor. The Coleman stove not only made the tea water hot, but it also warmed up the room which felt good to all of us.

After the tea and some canned soup, we rolled out the sleeping bags. The airplane had been safely secured for the night.

Suddenly, someone asked, "What about closing the flight plan? Will Search and Rescue be looking for us?"

"That's right," I said. "We will have to take fifteen-minute turns calling PAN on the radio." (PAN means you are in trouble but not in an emergency.)

"We hope some high-flying jetliner will hear us and relay a message to Fairbanks Flight Service. They need to be informed that we are all right and will be going to Northway in the morning if the weather is good for flying. Who will take the first fifteen-minute slot?" I asked.

Sharon, being an early-to-bed person, volunteered to be the first to call, "PAN, PAN, PAN. This is Cessna 206, C-FZNS stranded in the Yukon Mountains. We need someone to call Fairbanks Flight Service to cancel our flight plan."

Time dragged on and everyone was settled in except Judy, the night hawk. She volunteered to stay out in the plane to read a good book and call every fifteen minutes. About 2:30 a.m., Judy received a reply from a Japanese airliner. They had heard her message and confirmed that the message was relayed to Fairbanks Flight Service. Later we found out that Search and Rescue had been planning to send a helicopter to search for us first thing in the morning.

We had a good sleep. For breakfast we ate rolled oats and drank black tea from our survival kit. The rain had stopped and the weather was good for flying.

We loaded up and climbed into the airplane. Sharon was once again pilot-in-command for the upcoming flight. When she tried to start the airplane, the battery was dead! The two and a half hours on the radio the night before had drained the battery.

I had often hand propped the Cessna 206 over many years of flying, but there was not even enough life left in the battery to run the primer pump to start the engine. We took the battery out and heated it over a small fire because warmth gives it more life and power. When we thought it was warm enough, we put it back in the airplane. Sharon was in the pilot's seat. We carefully went over our starting procedure: throttle in one-fourth inch, boost pump on and be ready to turn on the master as I pull the propeller through for the start. It all went according to the plan except when the engine started Sharon turned off the boost pump too soon. Sharon worked the throttle, but the engine coughed and quit.

What a letdown! We went through the whole procedure again. We revived the fire to warm up the battery once more. Back to the airplane we went to install the battery again, hoping it would have enough life to run the boost pump one more time.

During our predicament Clara and one of the girls were praying about our situation. Everything was ready. I pulled the propeller through again and Sharon was at the controls. The boost pump ran long enough to start the engine. We were all thankful the engine kept running this time. The alternator was charging the battery! That created a lot of excitement for us.

Mary remembers how she and two of her sisters were exploring more of the abandoned buildings when the engine started. They knew they would need to hurry back to the airplane, so two bigger sisters each took an arm and dragged her to the airplane. In the process, one arm was sprained, creating a lot of pain for her.

After caring for Mary, we took off, knowing that later, her arm would need more careful attention. Sharon was pilot-in-command for the flight to Northway. She did an excellent takeoff keeping the nose wheel right on the dirt bike trail. Soon we were airborne and on our way to Northway.

As we gained some altitude, we were able to talk to a radio ground station. The operator was relieved to hear that we were airborne. There had been phone calls between Canada and Alaska about sending a Search and Rescue plane, because the morning hours were going by and there had been no word from the Cessna 206 C-FZNS.

We arrived at Northway, did U.S. Customs, refueled and had some breakfast at a quaint little frontier-looking restaurant. After breakfast we flew around a number of mountains on our way to Glenallen. When we arrived, Dwayne King met us.

> *I remember how thankful the U.S. Customs official was to welcome us to the U.S. It made us feel cared for.*
>
> *– Clara*

One of the first priorities was to take Mary to the hospital. She was well-cared for and her arm has been fine since that occasion. We enjoyed the people at Alaska Bible College in Glenallen and the Youth Seminar went well.

> *Life Lesson* CLARA AND I LEARNED
> AGAIN THAT WORKING
> TOGETHER HAS A
> PROFOUND POSITIVE EFFECT UPON THE CHILDREN.
> FATHERS AND MOTHERS WHO WORK TOGETHER IN
> CONCERT GENERALLY HAVE BETTER-BEHAVED CHILDREN
> WHO WILL CONTRIBUTE MORE TO SOCIETY.

• • •

There was another incident that happened over those mountains in the Piper Seneca II. Elaine Yoder was along on that trip to take pictures. On the last leg of our trip to Glenallen, Clara suggested that Elaine sit up front with me to take some good pictures of the majestic mountains. It was a beautiful, clear day and the mountains were spectacular.

Just as we were crossing a 10,000-foot mountain, the right engine began to push oil out of the front of the engine. I quickly shut down that engine and the propeller stood still. I started a slow descent into Glenallen. I said, "Elaine, take a picture of that propeller standing still." There was no response. I looked at her face and it was ashen white. She seemed frozen in time and space.

"Are you scared?" I asked. She nodded her head, yes. I explained that we could see the valley where the airport was located and that the other engine would take us there with no problem. Finally she relaxed enough to take a picture of the propeller stopped over the mountains. Within ten minutes we landed and discovered that the front oil seal had come out. In a few hours we had it fixed because Dwayne had an extra oil seal on hand. We were excited and thankful to be able to continue our trip to Anchorage, Alaska.

•   •   •

Sometime later we were in Alaska in the winter to teach Family Life Seminars. We had the Piper Seneca II twin engine plane on that trip. My daughters had never received their twin-engine rating. It was not that they could not have, because two of them were flying right seat and doing a good job. But they had teacher's or nurse's training or other educational pursuits they wanted to follow.

Thank you, Dad, for letting us go.
— Sharon

During our time in Alaska that winter, we taught Family Life Seminars in a number of communities. We went to Unalakleet, Nome, White Mountain, Kotzebue, Kivalina and Fairbanks.

In Kotzebue we had finished the last day of the Seminar about 4 p.m. We wanted to go about eighty miles up the coast to Kivalina. The coast lines are usually flat.

This was probably the worst mistake and misjudgment I made since I crashed the Piper J-3 Cub at my 200-hour mark, when I was twenty-six. By this time I had about 8500 hours of flying time and it is embarrassing to write this story, but perhaps someone can learn from it.

This was to be a short trip to Kivalina. By then I had my night rating. Darkness came at about 5 p.m. By 4:40 p.m. we were loaded, preflight had been done and we were airborne. I had not looked at the map. It would be a dusk-to-night flight at 1500 feet above the coastline. This should be an uneventful flight. We were out of Kotezbue about ten minutes and it was becoming dark and hazy. I thought we should soon see the lights of Kivalina.

But suddenly, I saw trees only a few feet below the Seneca II! Immediately I pushed all power to max and pulled the yoke right into my lap. That Seneca II climbed to 4500 feet fast! I really did not know what was around me or what had happened. I realized that I made a major mistake to plan a coastline dusk-to-night flight without checking my maps even though it was only sixty-five miles.

I was flying northwest along the coast to Kivalina where there was a beacon for locating the airport. But those trees I saw in the dusk just six feet below us and the instant sharp climb said one thing to me. Something was very, very wrong. There was only one thing to do—climb higher and make a 180° turn back to Kotzebue in a southeast direction.

Almost makes me cry to read this, even though I was not along.

— Sharon

I called Kotzebue radio and said, "I am returning to Kotzebue for the night." The Kotzebue radio operator wondered if I knew there were 2000-foot mountains about one-third of the way to Kivalina. By that time I did, so I was able to respond positively about the mountains in the area.

I returned to Kotzebue, landed and taxied into the parking place. I let my adrenaline subside and made new promises to myself never to assume anything and to always check everything, every time.

> *I can still see those trees.*
>
> *— Cathie*

A few minutes later I was about recovered from the whole ordeal when Cathie, who was sitting behind the co-pilot's seat on the right-hand side of the airplane on that flight, said, "Dad, why did you fly so close to that mountain? The right wing tip was nearly touching the mountain. The mountain just whizzed by the right wing tip just before you made that steep climb and did the 180° turn back to Kotzebue."

"Dear, I was looking out the left side. I didn't see the mountain," I replied.

I was jolted back into another adrenaline rush. It was clear to all of us by then that we had been very close to the Final Flight. We didn't even know how serious it was until it was all over. That would have been six funerals at once.

The fear I felt in the pit of my stomach that night is with me on almost every flight. I have always

> *I had not wanted to take off that evening, so late in the day. After we were in our bedroom that night, Clair apologized to me. He said, "We are a team. Your feelings and ideas are as important as mine. I promise you I will never do any flying when you don't feel comfortable going." He has kept that promise.*
>
> *— Clara*

said that I am a fearful pilot—a healthy sense of fear, but this event made that healthy fear stronger.

It took another few minutes for my adrenaline to settle. Then we thanked God for watching over us when we did not even know we were heading into a very dangerous situation.

Life Lesson ONE IMPORTANT LESSON FROM THAT EXPERIENCE WAS THAT I DID NOT KNOW HOW LOST I WAS UNTIL AFTERWARDS, WHEN I WAS ABLE TO LOOK BACK AND SEE WHERE I HAD BEEN AND WHAT TERRIBLE DESTRUCTION I WAS HEADED FOR, ALONG WITH MY WIFE AND FOUR OF MY DAUGHTERS.

SPIRITUALLY, I DID NOT KNOW AT NINETEEN YEARS OF AGE HOW BAD AND REBELLIOUS I WAS UNTIL I GAVE MY LIFE TO CHRIST AND WAS FORGIVEN FOR MY REBELLION AND MY WRONGDOINGS.

PANAMA ISLANDS— THE KUNA TRIBE

Lino Smith is a member of the Kuna Tribe who live on the islands off the northeast coast of Panama. They maintain fields and gardens on the flats at the foot of the mountains and travel to and from their gardens in dugout canoes.

At a conference in Texas I met Lino Smith who was a translator and spoke fluent Kuna, Spanish and English. He was an outgoing man who loved life, his family and his people. Lino requested that we bring the Family Life Seminar to the Kuna people so he could translate the material and make it appropriate for them.

By that time I was flying the Seneca II with Seneca III engines. The plane was also equipped with a stall kit and vortex generators to reduce the landing speed. It was an excellent performer with low landing speeds and good takeoff and climb performance.

Dorcas (our secretary), Clara and I flew the Seneca II down through Mexico and Central America. That was no real problem because we had previously been to Belize, Mexico, El Salvador, Haiti and the Dominican Republic.

When we arrived in Panama City, we connected with Lino. The next day he and I made a trip to five small islands to test the runways. Lino also wanted to inform the people about the upcoming Family Life Seminars.

The first runway was made of long bamboo poles laid in a swampy area. The 1800-foot runway ran east to west from the foot of the mountain to the Caribbean Sea.

On my first try, I flew down the mountain toward the runway. On the flareout I realized I had too much speed, so I opted for a go-around. On the climb-out, Lino said, "You must sideslip the plane down the mountain so you will not be going so fast for landing."

Sideslip the Seneca II down the mountain? I thought to myself. Years earlier I had done a good number of sideslips with the Piper J-3, but a slideslip with the twin-engine Seneca II seemed questionable.

I made a large circuit to process the whole scenario, because if I went off the other end of the runway, we would be in the Caribbean Sea and that wasn't a good option! At the top of the mountain I set a nice, slow sideslip down the mountain. Just before landing, I leveled out and set the Seneca II on the bamboo runway. We stopped just past the midway point. It wasn't too bad after all with the flying tips from my Kuna interpreter. I decided to do it another time to practise before I brought the loaded airplane in the next day. It was fun and challenging!

The next island had a 1200-foot cement runway running north to south, with the Caribbean Sea at each end. As I circled, I reviewed the approach speeds and landing speeds and checked the wind. I was certain I had to set the plane down on the first fifty feet of runway to have enough runway to stop. And I did it with 200 feet to spare!

When we were finished for the day, Lino wanted to stop at the tourist island to buy some lobsters for supper. The runway was 1500 feet long, but it had a washout at the 1200-foot point on the south end. I flew a long approach to set up everything and fly by the numbers. As we were taxiing to the lobster place, a well-dressed, handsome, official-looking man came walking across the grass. I was a bit nervous, wondering what I might have done wrong.

When we climbed out of the airplane, he shook our hands and introduced himself as the Minister of Aviation of Panama. I was wondering, *What next?*

He looked at me and asked, "You're the pilot?"

"Yes, sir," I replied.

"I watched you land," he continued. "You are an excellent pilot. I wish I could hire pilots like you here in Panama."

"Thank you," I said.

"Have a good time in Panama." I assured him we would.

Lino bought the lobsters and we returned to Panama City for a delicious lobster supper.

We spent nearly two weeks on the islands. The teachings were well received. We had a ride in a dugout canoe and also had some delicious roasted wild pig and other local food.

The last place where we were to be for several days was the southernmost island near Colombia. As soon as we arrived, men began measuring the airplane with a long vine. I asked Lino what they were doing. He explained that three missionaries had been captured by guerillas just across the Colombian border. Lino went on to explain that the men were going to cut out a hole in the jungle to hide the airplane. They had arranged for men to guard the airplane around the clock. Lino and his people were so appreciative of our coming that they wanted to make things as safe as possible. The Seneca II looked rather cozy in its jungle "hangar."

However, during our stay there, the Seneca II wheels settled in the fresh, soft sand of the recently cleared jungle floor. Many people were required to pull on a long rope to move the plane to the grass runway. We joked about "Kuna power."

I agree.
– Clara

This time with the Kuna people was the best and most enjoyable flying and teaching of my career. The Kuna people took good care of us.

8

GEAR-UP LANDINGS

I finished Chapter Six with the worst mistake that I ever made. However, the two gear-up landings I will describe next were not caused by pilot error but by mechanical problems.

Nonetheless, landing on the belly of the airplane and hearing the propellers grinding themselves to ruins in gravel and ice is certainly not a pleasant experience. Any pilot knows the airplane will be down for a while.

My training in retractable gear flying was excellent. The final check is "three in the green; one in the mirror." That simply means that the pilot has three green lights, one green light on the dash for each of the three wheels. A green light means the wheels are down and locked in place. "One in the mirror" means the pilot can actually see the nose wheel by a mirror that is installed on the pilot's side of the airplane.

On the first incident I had about 8500 hours of flying time, with 2000 hours in the Seneca II. We were in Alaska doing seminars in various communities on the north slopes of the Brooks Range and along the coast of the Arctic Ocean.

Anaktuvuk Pass was the next stop for teaching on family life. The community is located in a wide valley between two mountains. The actual pass is much narrower and is several miles up the big valley.

At Anaktuvuk Pass the airport was in a nice location, had plenty of length and was well maintained. There were airport lights and an airport beacon which provided guidance for landing.

On my downwind leg of the circuit, I put the landing gear handle down. The red light went off, but the three green lights did not come on. I tried to raise the gear, but they would not come up. In the mirror the nose wheel was visible but didn't seem to be in a down and locked position. The gear were down too far for the manual free-fall lock system to work.

It did not seem right to stay in the air until I ran out of fuel in one and a half hours. Neither would it help to go to another airport, because none I could think of would be any

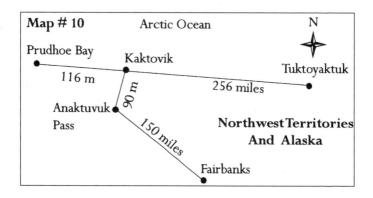

better than this one, so I opted to land and see if the gear might be locked without the green lights being on for some unknown reason.

As I landed I could feel the wheels fold up into the belly of the plane. I could hear the propellers chewing up the gravel. The four propeller blades were being destroyed. The airplane slid on the belly before coming to a stop. I breathed a big sigh of relief. The words of George Lore came back to my mind, "Clair, any landing you can walk away from is a good landing."

Several men came out to help jack up the airplane. Once it was jacked up, the gear came part way down. We were able to pull them into the locked position. There sat the airplane on three wheels. The main visible damage was the curled up propeller blades.

The men towed the plane into the parking area. I phoned the insurance company, and they worked out a plan to have two other usable propellers flown in so I could ferry the airplane out to Fairbanks for repairs. I did that trip with the wheels down and locked. In Fairbanks the airplane was put into a hangar for repairs. First the mechanics had to find the problem.

I did not experience this with Clair. I was at another community waiting for him to return. But I was thankful when he called to say that he was safe.

– Clara

The reason for the gear failure was soon discovered. The main electrical control unit on the left gear leg was shorted out and the pieces were burned together. That locked up the whole

Life Lesson THERE ARE TIMES WE
MUST ACCEPT THE GOOD
WITH THE BAD. LIFE HAS MANY MYSTERIES. MANY PEOPLE
FIND IT HARD TO LIVE WITH MYSTERY. SOME PEOPLE FEEL
THEY MUST HAVE AN ANSWER FOR EVERYTHING. IT IS BEST
NOT TO TRY TO OUTGUESS GOD, OR LIVE ON "IF ONLYS."

electrical system for all three wheels. It must have shorted out when the gear was down and almost in the locked position.

The engines were taken apart to see if the crankshafts were bent or broken from the propellers grinding in the gravel. The engine shop had good news and bad news. The good news was that the crankshafts were not bent. The bad news was that, in the right engine, they found the main bearing mounting broken off from the engine case.

This problem had nothing to do with the gear incident. It was an altogether different problem. The engine mechanic said it was good I had had the gear problem so that the engine problem could be discovered.

The mechanics felt that the engine would have gone to pieces during one of the next flights. In one way, that is not too serious because a Seneca II flies well with only one engine. However, the plane cannot maintain the higher altitudes for mountainous areas with only one engine running.

My Grandpa always said, "Every cloud has a silver lining." This was our silver lining.

The mechanic said, "Your gear problem was really minor

compared to what could have happened if that right engine had gone to pieces with gross weight over a 10,000-foot mountain."

We acquired and installed two new motors and two freshly overhauled propellers, which enabled us to continue our ministry.

The second gear-up landing was on an ice road three miles from the Yellowknife airport. An ice road is a roadway plowed across a frozen lake, often to new mining sites or a logging camp.

The airplane had just come back from a repair shop near Harrisburg, Pennsylvania. Each wing had had BF Goodrich fuel bladders replaced, because the old ones had started to leak.

It was wintertime when Clara and I headed for Inuvik, Tuktoyaktuk and Sachs Harbour, Northwest Territories. We had left Dryden the day before and stopped at Thompson, Manitoba, for fuel and overnight lodging.

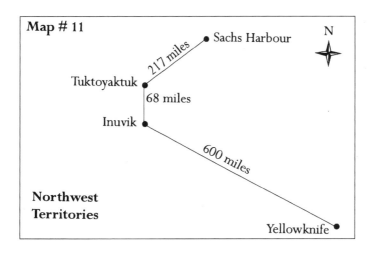

The next morning we left Thompson for Yellowknife. As we were approaching Yellowknife, we should have had another one and one-half hours of fuel in the main tanks. But something did not seem right about the fuel gauges on both engines. During the preflight check at Thompson, I had opened both gas caps to see if the fuel man had filled the tanks. The tanks were full to the top.

At this time both gauges were bobbing on empty, but according to time calculations and fuel consumption per hour, that did not seem right.

The airport was only three miles away. I radioed the Yellowknife airport tower and was cleared to land. We were nearly over the town of Yellowknife when both engines quit only seconds apart. It seemed so unbelievable! I was at circuit altitude of 1000 feet. I could clearly see the runway one and one-half to two miles in front of me, but just behind us was a widely plowed ice road to a mining operation.

Trying for the runway would probably mean ending up short, on top of one of the houses. That didn't seem to be a good option, so I immediately made a 180° turn back toward the ice road away from the community. The ice road was approximately one-eighth of a mile away on the snow-covered lake with no houses nearby.

I did a quick pre-landing check. Gear down? No, because if I did not make the ice road, I would be landing in deep snow. I could hear what mechanics said many times: "If you are landing in the trees or deep snow or whatever, keep the gear up. There will be less damage to the airplane. If the wheels are down and ripped out of the wings, you have major internal damage to both wings."

When you are at 1000 feet with a twin engine aircraft, you must make decisions in split seconds. I opted to keep the gear up, because the ice road seemed just a little far away for the glide distance I figured I had left. We did make the ice road just over the snowbank, but there was no time to drop the gear and land straight and level.

I was in a right turn to make it over the snowbank and to line up with the road. I quickly pushed some left rudder to line up the airplane to stay on the ice road. A car was coming towards us. The ice road was plowed as wide as a six-lane highway. The frightened lady driver did a 180° turn and sped away! In one way it was funny because when we stopped sliding on the belly, we were still some distance from where she had turned around. One thing is for sure: she had probably never seen an airplane sliding down the ice road before and hopefully never has since.

I awoke at this point in time. I was confused as to why Clair was flying so low. He looked calm. I didn't say a word. It was good I didn't distract him. When we slid along on the road I became wide awake!

– Clara

When the airplane came to a stop, we could see the curled propellers. Everything else seemed to be in good condition. Clara and I sat and looked at each other in utter amazement. The whole trip ended in a way we had not planned, but we were safe.

Then came the time for the decision, how do we move the airplane to the airport? I remembered that we had bought the Seneca II from a road construction company in Yellowknife. The call letters of Seneca C-GRTH would mean something to them if I called them on the cell phone.

Before long, the police, the ambulance, the fire department and the environmentalists were there. The radio and TV men were there, too. We became the center of attention at Yellowknife.

The ambulance people had to be assured that Clara and I were fine. Finally they left. Then the police left. The fire trucks left when the firemen realized that there was no chance of fire. The environmentalists were the hardest to convince that there were no fuel leaks or spills. Finally they left.

The news people stayed around so they could obtain the story of which we knew very little, except that the airplane had run out of fuel one and one-half hours before it should have.

The people at Tuktoyaktuk, Northwest Territories, saw me on the news on TV.
– Clara

Of course they wondered what had happened. I explained that I simply did not know why we were short on fuel. I told them I had checked the tanks on the pre-flight check at Thompson. I assured them that the tanks had been filled to the top. The normal time for the amounts of fuel was so many hours and so many minutes, but the rest was mystery until further investigation. The more important task was to arrange for and move the airplane to the airport.

By this time the previous owner had driven up. He heard Seneca II C-GRTH on his radio and had recognized by the call sign that this was the airplane he had sold to someone in Dryden, Ontario. He came to discuss a plan to move the airplane to the airport. What a wonderful surprise!

He decided on a plan to send a truck for the luggage and boxes in the plane to make it as light as possible, and he immediately radioed for the truck.

The next part of the plan was to bring out a big hoist truck to lift the airplane so we could drop the gear and load the airplane on a low bed truck and haul it to the airport.

"The big Caterpiller tractor is already clearing an ice road around Yellowknife to the airport," he said.

The hoist truck and the low bed were there in a short time. Within one hour the airplane was sitting by a big hangar on a trailer. I thanked the previous owner profusely, because he and the other men had done a marvelous job. We were so appreciative.

Then I called the insurance company. They eventually found two propellers and had the engines taken apart and checked. The mechanics found everything else to be in good condition.

Clara and I arranged for the Cessna 206 to be brought for us to use for the rest of that trip. But the big mystery still remained: where was the fuel? Upon further investigation, the mechanics discovered that the new fuel bladders were not installed according to the BF Goodrich's instructions. The top of the bladders were to be fastened at the top with velcro to cleaned metal. The instructions clearly said: "Fasten the velcro to the aluminum after a thorough cleaning."

Instead of following the instructions, the mechanic had lined the top of the inside of the wing with duct tape and then glued the velcro to the duct tape. The duct tape did not stick to the aluminum and, therefore, in certain places it came loose which allowed parts of the fuel bladder to drop down. This reduced the fuel capacity by 28 gallons on each side.

The bladder tank was fastened by a ring of small bolts around the filling cap. So the tank looked full upon visual inspection at the fuel cap. The dropped parts of the top of the bladders could not be seen from the fuel filling opening.

The Canadian repair shop did the proper bladder installation. We never had any more problems with those tanks. One lesson I learned from this was to always estimate the amount of fuel used on a specific trip and compare that with the actual fuel taken on board. (I had been taught that procedure, but over time, forgot it.)

One day after that incident, my wife did some calculating. If that problem had not been discovered, two days later we could very well have been set up for a story with a much different ending.

If we had reached the Yellowknife airport, we would have refueled and flown on to Inuvik and Tuktoyaktuk, towns further north in the Northwest Territories.

From Tuktoyaktuk, we were planning to fly to Sachs Harbour with four more people. At Sachs Harbour, the approach to the airport is over an expanse of very cold, icy waters of the Northwest Passage. The way the currents travel, there is usually open water on the approach path to the most used runway at Sachs Harbour.

In retrospect, the shocking thing is that if the engines would have experienced fuel starvation at that point, all six of us would have gone into the icy water. Not one of the six of us would have been rescued alive. We would have all drowned in the cold, icy waters of the Northwest Passage.

Praise the Lord for a different ending!
– Carolyn

In both cases there was little or no damage to the airframe. Both times the propellers were damaged beyond repair. The second time the engines had to be taken apart to check for any internal damage and fortunately there was none.

Life Lesson AGAIN, MORE MYSTERY. WE HAVE MORE "WHY" QUESTIONS THAN ANSWERS. OUR LIVES ARE IN GOD'S HANDS. WE WILL CONTINUE FLYING TO HELP YOUTH AND FAMILIES.

9

Arctic Flying

The Arctic regions are often called the barren lands, but the Arctic is *not* barren. In the summer there are thousands and thousands of beautiful flowers, lovely birds, interesting rocks and many clear, blue lakes. A walk or canoe trip in the Arctic summer is an awesome experience.

The Arctic winters have their own beauty, but one must beware of polar bears. They are a majestic and magnificent sight to behold. The polar bears are not the same as the black bears of the south, who are as scared of people as many people are scared of them. Polar bears attack people. A man or a woman is no match for the strength and hunger of the polar bear of the Arctic.

The severe cold temperatures are just as deadly if one is not dressed properly. Dressing for the Arctic winters can be learned best by having someone who was born and raised there teach you how to dress properly. You must use much natural material such as furs, tanned hides and goose down. Some of the new synthetic materials are proving to be very useful also. But it is the people of the Arctic who teach others how to dress, so that they can really enjoy the cold temperatures and Arctic blizzards.

Clara and I love to walk in a blizzard. There is something invigorating about the majestic, strong and challenging Arctic blizzards. But we need to be dressed properly or those blizzards can kill just as quickly as polar bears.

In July 1967 a friend of mine, Harold Fly, and I made a trip with a Luscombe 8F to Gillam and Churchill, Manitoba, and Eskimo Point (now renamed Arviat), Whale Cove and Rankin Inlet, Nunavut, to explore the need for Youth and Family Life Seminars in the Arctic. That was an interesting excursion in a small, two-place Luscombe on floats.

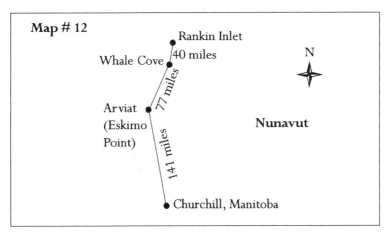

From Churchill to Eskimo Point, it was easy to follow the maps along the western coast of Hudson Bay. Many little lakes and inlets from Hudson Bay provided navigational points on the maps. On that trip we discovered a desire from the people for Youth and Family Life Seminars.

Clara and I were so busy in southern Canada that we could not arrange for Youth or Family Seminars in the Arctic until the winter of 1976, a decade later. A Youth Seminar was arranged for the community of Arviat in February 1976. I spent some time on the phone with the pastor, David Caskey, about what types of clothing we should be wearing, so we could be well prepared.

We made this trip in the Cessna 206 on wheels. We stopped at Gillam and Churchill for fuel, just as we had done ten years before in the Luscombe 8F.

The stretch from Churchill to Arviat proved to be a difficult flight. The lakes and the Hudson Bay coastline were frozen and snow-covered. It was one of those gray days without sunshine. Here and there some of the larger rocks could be seen, which provided enough positioning spots for the flight. Under those conditions, I could understand how a pilot could easily lose any sense of a horizon and become completely disoriented, ending up in a downward spiral into the ground. Winter visual references for navigation were very difficult to find. It was much different than summer flying.

On that trip I determined to obtain my instrument flight training (IFR) and certification before I made any more winter flights in the Arctic.

I knew that my family needed some first-hand experience in simple igloo building on the cold winter tundra. Sometimes motors on airplanes do quit. Emergencies could happen that would put us on the wintery tundra overnight or longer.

The day before the seminar started, our family planned three hours out on the cold tundra. We had Mr. Caskey show us a snow knife and demonstrate how it was used. He taught us the basic principles of building a wall or an igloo to provide some shelter against the cold Arctic winds. Mr. Caskey had assured us that no polar bears were around that winter! We wanted to know that before we went out.

I remember going out.
— Sharon

By this time the family members who were along could clearly understand the sense of it all. We bundled up in all our Arctic clothing. Mr. Caskey took us by snow machine and sled approximately one mile from town.

He showed us how to draw a circle in the wind-driven, hard-packed Arctic snow. He explained that you cut the snow blocks from inside the circle and stack them around the circle so that you are going both up and down as you build. This provides quicker shelter from the Arctic winds.

Being out in the Arctic wind and in the real Arctic environment made a lot of sense to all of us. The idea was to build a wind-proof wall as soon as possible for the youngest one to have a warmer place with Clara.

Ten minutes later I told Mr. Caskey that he could go home for two hours. With our sleeping bags and with the snow knife we would be all right. I used the snow knife and the girls set up snow blocks. Soon Clara was able to sit down behind the wall with five-year-old Mary Lois.

The hole became deeper and the wall grew higher. In time some of the other girls joined Clara and Mary Lois. They cuddled up behind the wall in sleeping bags. Just being out of the wind was a relief.

I kept cutting blocks and the rest of the girls kept placing them. On the third round the girls began to pull the circle in to begin to form a round roof. We filled the cracks with snow. We never did finish the complete igloo, especially the side away from the wind.

As a small child, this trip stands out in my memory. I remember my green snowsuit, my blue, sheep-lined mittens and my frost-bitten nose. I also have memories of warm, cozy houses, warm friendly people and enjoying eating raw, frozen caribou meat with my dad. My family thought I was brave.

– Mary

When Mr. Caskey came back, some of us were making black tea on the Coleman stove we had brought along. The others were all curled up in the thick down sleeping bags. We were actually quite comfortable by the time Mr. Caskey arrived for us. In this way we gained some first-hand experience surviving in the Arctic winter.

The seminars went well. We enjoyed the families as we taught the Youth and Family material. We established some friendships that continue more than thirty years later.

Our trip home was rather uneventful. We had had our first Arctic experience and survived.

The next week I phoned the Winnipeg Flying Club to arrange for my instrument flight training after more than twenty years as a bush pilot.

• • •

One winter our family went to Alaska with the Cessna 206. Our daughters did many hours of left-seat flying through mountain passes and along the river systems. The Yukon River is an excellent river to follow.

"It is beginning to snow lightly," Judy said as we flew through one mountain pass. "We have no idea what might be in the narrowest part of the pass. To avoid any chance of white-out conditions, I think we should do a 180° turn and head back to the airport we passed about ten minutes ago."

"A good call. There is no point in trying something that is dangerous," I replied.

In a few hours we tried it again and everything was clear. We arrived safely and were able to start the Family Life Seminar by 7 p.m.

Later on that trip we followed the Dempster Highway from Dawson City, Yukon, to Inuvik, Northwest Territories. After refueling at Inuvik we went on to Tuktoyaktuk. A week later when leaving Tuktoyaktuk, Sharon was flying left seat as pilot-in-command. The sky was clear, but the wind was blowing across the taxiway. The taxiway lights and markers were hard to see.

Sharon went close to the right snowbank. The soft snow pulled us into the snowbank. The propeller sprayed snow in every direction. Sharon cut the power. All but Sharon and little Mary Lois crawled out to push the airplane back onto the taxiway.

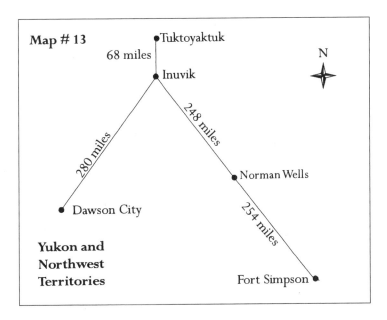

One propeller blade had a nasty nick in it from some gravel in the snowbank. I found my file. I always try to be prepared, because often you are the only weatherman and the only mechanic. Soon the propeller was filed according to specifications.

We all crawled back in and Sharon taxied out to the runway. As soon as the airplane reached the runway, the visibility improved because the snow was blowing from the west straight down the runway. All the runway lights were visible, even in the daytime. After taxiing to the end of the runway, she took off and we were airborne on our way down the Mackenzie River to the town of Norman Wells, Northwest Territories, where we stopped for fuel and breakfast. The next stop was Fort Simpson, Northwest Territories, where we did another seminar.

Three days later we made a fast trip from Fort Simpson to Winnipeg with one fuel stop in a little over six hours of flying time with the Cessna 206! At 9500 feet we had a 95-knot tailwind. It was good we were not flying northwest that day; we would have had to stop several times for fuel. The girls would have had much time to do schoolwork or to be bored.

• • •

On another trip the next winter, we landed for fuel at Coppermine (Kugluktuk), Nunavut, on the Northwest Passage. It was a clear day and I was pilot-in-command. The winds were much stronger than forecasted. It was an exact crosswind. The community and the airport buildings were visible, but the runway was not. I asked for the runway lights and strobes to be turned on full bright, but I still couldn't see the runway.

By this time I had my instrument flight training, so I did the instrument approach over the airport beacon. On the final approach path, the needle on my instrument showed I was crabbing appropriately in the crosswind for a straight-in landing. At 450 feet I could see the strobe lights and the runway lights. We landed without difficulty. With years of practice, crosswind landings can be challenging and safe.

From Coppermine we went to Cambridge Bay for a week of meetings. Then we headed for Churchill, Manitoba, but had to stop at Baker Lake for fuel. At Baker Lake, the wind was strong and right down the runway at 45 mph. The Cessna 206 lands at 45 mph, because a Horton Stall Kit had been installed. When we landed, the airplane was sitting still! After refueling, we went on our way.

We arrived at Churchill in good time to begin the Youth Seminar. Here there was almost no wind and it was a beautiful sunny day. It was almost too nice to fly! After the teaching

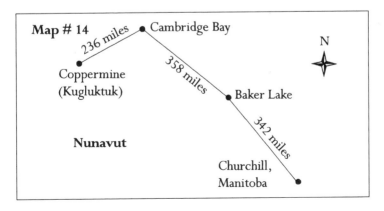

sessions that evening, we had raw, frozen, thinly-sliced caribou meat with black tea.

The Arctic is a great place to fly, but if one is going to fly in the Arctic, it is important to talk with other experienced pilots to learn all one can.

LEARNING TO FLY
IN THE CLOUDS

After hearing the following story I was determined to take IFR (Instrument Flight Rules) training. Too much was at stake if I did not take the training and obtain the certification.

I heard of a bush pilot who started out flying in a little two-seater airplane with no starter, generator or radio—just as I had done. The pilot always had to start the airplane by swinging the propeller by hand, with one hand on the door post and the other on the propeller. One foot was placed in front of the wheel to block it. Prior to swinging the prop by hand the priming was done, the magnetos turned on and the throttle set.

This pilot I heard about did obtain his commercial license and bought a Cessna 185. He began a small air charter service. Everything was going well hauling people and freight in and out of many fishing and hunting camps.

Later, he added a Beaver airplane to his fleet. He hired more pilots. Finally, he bought a new twin-engine airplane for the growing airport business. This new twin had many instruments on the panel and was fully equipped for IFR flying. He had accumulated well over 12,000 hours of successful bush flying.

People told him that he ought to do his IFR training and obtain IFR certification. They said, "The new airplane is fully equipped with instruments you have never been trained to use."

His usual response was, "I have been doing well for 12,000 hours. Why should I bother taking the time for IFR certification? I always get the trips made."

But one day he was flying several businessmen from one airport to another. At one point he radioed for the current weather at the destination airport. He told them that it was snowing heavily where he was and he may need to turn back. At the destination airport the skies were overcast, but it had not yet begun to snow.

There was no further contact. The airplane did not arrive at the destination airport, nor did it return to the airport of origin. Two hours later Search and Rescue began looking for the crash site. Soon after the search began they picked up an Emergency Locator Transmitter (ELT) transmitting beeps on the emergency frequency.

Search and Rescue homed in on the signal and found the airplane crashed upside down on the ice in the middle of a big lake. The pilot and businessmen were killed in that crash.

Apparently the snowfall had increased and the pilot had tried to turn back but flew into a whiteout over the snow-covered lake. It was assumed that he had lost all outside visual references and went into a right or left downward spiral. The end was fatal and final. One foot in front of his eyes was everything he needed to conduct that flight safely, but he never felt it necessary for anyone to train him to use those excellent instruments.

So sad! So needless!

THIS IS SIMILAR TO PEOPLE WHO WON'T READ THE BIBLE OR HAVE ANYONE TEACH THEM HOW TO LIVE IN A GODLY MANNER. THEN THEY WONDER WHY THEY DRANK SO MUCH AND BECAME SICK WITH CIRRHOSIS OF THE LIVER; OR WHY THEY SMOKED SO MUCH AND ARE DYING OF LUNG CANCER; OR WHY THEIR MARRIAGE BROKE UP; OR WHY THEIR GROWN CHILDREN GET INTO SO MUCH TROUBLE.

By now you have some glimpse of the necessity of learning to fly IFR in the clouds and snowy weather. There are many "whiteout" conditions in the Arctic in the winter on gray days when the earth, sky and everything in between looks the same. A pilot can easily lose the horizon, and that is why IFR training is valuable. I have heard of too many pilots who were not trained to fly in whiteout conditions and simply spiralled to their deaths.

The other advantage of IFR training is that a pilot can fly over some weather systems that would make flying by Visual Flight Rules (VFR) impossible.

Finally the time had arrived for me to begin my IFR flight training at the Winnipeg Flying Club located at the St. Andrews Airport about fifteen miles north of Winnipeg. There were several pilots in the class. All of us were experienced bush pilots with over 6000 hours of total flight time.

In the beginning of the course we were told that training an experienced bush pilot to fly IFR is more difficult than training a new pilot with fewer hours and preferably no bush time.

In IFR flying, the maps are clearly marked to show how low the pilot can fly and be 1000 to 2000 feet above the highest obstacle. This way the pilot can choose his altitude and fly through the clouds from one radio navigational aid to the next one without ever seeing the ground.

The airport landing charts are also clearly marked as to directions of flight and altitudes that lead the pilot on the final approach path to the runway. If the airport and runway are not visible due to blowing snow, heavy snow or fog, the charts also show how low the pilot can descend before he declares a missed approach and applies full power to climb up again. On a missed approach a pilot must always have plans for a suitable alternate airport.

At that point the pilot has to decide whether he is going to attempt another landing or fly to the designated alternate airport where the weather forecast must be better.

Before the flight, the pilot needs to select the altitudes and the flight path and put the information into his flight plan, so air traffic controllers can keep proper separation between air traffic.

When doing IFR flying, the airplane must be equipped with a transponder. A transponder sends out signals for radar to read. The code consists of four numbers as assigned to the pilot before departure by air traffic controllers who are responsible for the separation of air traffic.

All this makes it extremely important to fly the headings and altitudes and keep using the transponder code. The pilot keeps that transponder code operating during climbout and on every part of the flight until he has landed. After the pilot has landed, he must report when he is clear of the runway so the air traffic controllers can close the IFR flight plan.

In the event of landing at an uncontrolled airport where there may be no radio operators, the pilot must make an immediate phone call to notify the air traffic control center that he has landed, and then close the flight plan.

The experienced bush pilot has learned well how to fly his plane in many kinds of weather conditions—often with no radio contact—at least back in the early days. A bush pilot has learned to trust himself and his abilities. No one talked to him about what to do next. It was all up to him.

Bush pilots are usually confident, self-assured, do-it-alone, and tough. In bush flying it is the pilot and the airplane. A bush pilot had to fly and care for the airplane by himself in all kinds of good, not-so-good and bad circumstances.

Some have said, "It was the pilot, the airplane and luck." Others, such as I, said, "It was the pilot, the airplane and God."

Our IFR instructor told us right up front that we would need to go through some personality change and would need to learn to trust the instruments in front of our faces. Before IFR training, bush pilots used some of the instruments and some were just there. Only the instruments helpful for VFR flying were used (when they worked).

The instructor informed us, too, that we would need to become used to being told the direction of flight (headings), the altitude and sometimes the speed. We were told that we were used to depending on ourselves, but flying IFR meant that we would have to depend on air traffic controllers telling us what to do. Trust would be a major factor, thus the need for some personality adjustments!

Learning to trust the instruments in front of one's face, with no outside visual reference, is often difficult. Learning to trust air traffic controllers is another adjustment.

"Frankly," they said, "some bush pilots cannot make the adjustments. Others decide partway through the training just to continue being a good bush pilot and drop out of IFR training. Some work at the adjustment, stick with the program and become good IFR pilots."

Finally the day came for us to wear the hood, which was designed for us to see the instrument panel without any outside reference. It was indeed a strange feeling. I felt so closed in and out of control. The word "trust" kept ringing in my mind. My wife tells me that I did go through a personality change. She felt I became more gentle, more trusting, and less self-assured.

That's true.
– Clara

Eventually all of my classmates dropped out. Some couldn't handle it emotionally and others felt it was not worth the effort. They decided they would continue to be bush pilots. Several times I felt that I wanted to quit and that I could not adjust. Yet, I always heard the voice in my heart of people and families asking for more of the Youth, Family Life and Parenting Skills Seminars in the Arctic regions. Deep within me, I knew it was my calling to obtain my IFR training and certification.

So, I plugged on and on. The whole experience was exactly as I was told it would be. The question would often come back, "Why not quit?" I knew I could, but if I decided to quit, I did not know what to do with the internal voice and calling. I felt that I could not live with myself if I quit. The internal voice and the holy calling would always be there. The day eventually came for the final Ministry of Transport IFR test ride. I was very nervous but felt I had been well trained. I had learned to trust the instruments and flight controllers.

It was not a perfect ride, but it was a safe and acceptable one. I passed and received my IFR certification! To this day, I cannot explain the difference in feelings from the years before and the years after my IFR training.

I do know that after my IFR training I felt more sure about flying as a VFR pilot also. Now as an IFR pilot, I have confidence, but also a sense of trepidation that has made me a safer pilot. I have done the right thing by acquiring my IFR certificate.

•   •   •

As in the rest of my relationship with dad, my impressions of my dad as a pilot and what I experienced flying with him are complex. In my perfectionism, I was often worrying that he wasn't doing things by the book as I thought he should. However, I've admired his knowledge of all the ins and outs of bush flying, his ability in handling an airplane, his ability in dealing with the many situations that arise in northern flying, and his quick thinking and quick action in situations that required it. I can still thrill to stories that reflect that quick thinking and quick action. I've admired how he's been willing to acquire news skills in obtaining his IFR rating, and in learning how to fly a turbo-prop aircraft along with more safety routines that have accompanied the new skills.

— Judy

I remember an interesting incident when flying from Anchorage to McGrath, Alaska, on my first IFR trip in the Seneca II.

On the approach into McGrath, something was not lining up properly. We were in solid cloud. I remembered the words of my IFR instructors, "If something doesn't seem right on an approach, do a missed approach immediately." So I immediately did a missed approach and reported to McGrath radio, "Seneca II C-GRTH doing a missed approach. Will come around for another approach."

"RTH, McGrath radio, report over Initial Approach Fix inbound," the radio operator replied.

A few minutes later an incoming airliner requested approach clearance into McGrath. They were given a clearance to do the holding pattern at 8,000 feet over the radio beacon until a Seneca II on a missed approach reported down and clear.

On the second approach, everything was lining up properly. We landed and reported clear. The airliner was given his clearance to do his approach and land. When they landed, the passengers were mumbling about their delay due to a little guy doing a missed approach. They were saying that their pilot had reported on the intercom, "We are delayed landing clearance. We need to hold for a while until a little guy down there gets his act together."

They did not know my wife was sitting there while I was refueling. Later when I came in, Clara told me what the passengers were saying, and that she felt embarrassed. Clara and I discussed the situation. I explained it was better to do a missed approach than to continue an approach that was off-target. That was all part of learning to fly safely in the clouds. We all have a right to the skies and we all have a right to learn. Embarrassing, yes, somewhat, but better embarrassed than to fly into the side of a mountain. My wife wholeheartedly agreed.

Life Lesson DO NOT LET PUBLIC OPINION OR THE FEAR OF EMBARRASSMENT KEEP YOU FROM DOING THE RIGHT AND SAFE THING. IN FLYING, A PILOT MUST NOT GIVE IN TO THE PRESSURE OF OTHERS AND TRY SOMETHING THAT APPEARS TO BE UNSAFE.

11

Scary Times

"Dad, is this the right airport?" Sharon exclaimed as she poked me in the ribs to awaken me. "No one answers the radios and there is grass growing in the cracks of the concrete on the runway. I'm confused!"

We were on a flight with the Cessna 206 from Calgary, Alberta, to Cut Bank, Montana, where we were planning to do U.S. customs, buy some fuel and continue on our way to Hutchinson, Kansas. Sharon was pilot-in-command and she did a great job flying out of the big airport of Calgary. I was in the co-pilot's seat having a good nap, since it was a clear, calm day for flying.

I rubbed my eyes, looked around and saw no one at what was supposed to be the Cut Bank Municipal Airport. I quickly looked at the map and saw we were on the runway of an abandoned military base north of Cut

> It is good I poked you. At least I knew when to alert the boss.
>
> — Sharon

Bank. It was near the track to the Cut Bank Municipal Airport. The map did show the abandoned military airport but had "abandoned" in small letters.

"Sharon, this is the old abandoned military airport. The municipal airport is about another twenty miles on the same track," I exclaimed. "Give full power and let's get out of here, because we would be in big trouble landing in the U.S. without customs officials being present."

Sharon quickly understood the situation and pushed the throttle "to the wall" for a quick takeoff. The runway was 10,000 feet long, but we were airborne in less than 1000 feet.

She climbed to an altitude of 5500 feet and headed for Cut Bank Municipal Airport. Within a few minutes she was talking with the radio operators at Cut Bank airport. We landed and met the customs official who did not ask many questions or check anything. We refueled and had an uneventful flight to Hutchinson, Kansas.

Sharon learned without my having to say anything to look at the fine print and the big print on aviation maps.

•   •   •

Some years later we made a flight from Bella Coola, British Columbia, to the island of Bella Bella. I was the pilot-in-command because the girls wanted to rest. It had been a grueling trip up to that point. As well, the flight was through a mountain pass in the mountainous regions of the west coast of British Columbia to an island in the Pacific Ocean.

From Bella Coola to Bella Bella was a twenty-minute flight. The weather at Bella Bella was clear; the weather at Bella Coola was overcast at 2000 feet. In this short flight, we had to fly over a long inlet of water from the Pacific Ocean between mountains as high as 7000 feet. One never knows what to expect when flying between two mountains.

Seven or eight minutes out, the ceiling became lower and the wind increased in velocity. We were down to 500 feet above the huge ocean waves, and the turbulence became the worst I had ever experienced. The airplane bounced left and right and up and down. At one point we dropped suddenly and far enough that the heavy steel bases of the microphone stands (one foot in diameter) were floating at face level in the air inside the airplane.

I slowed the airplane to manoeuvring speed and hung on to the yoke to try to keep the Cessna 206 as straight and level as I could, but it was never straight or level. To make matters worse, my check points were not showing up along the shore as they should have been. The clouds came lower, so I had to descend to less than 500 feet above the huge waves in the severe turbulence.

Sharon told me later that she was resigned to dying. As far as she was concerned, she would soon be on her final flight into the heavenlies, as her body would sink into those huge waves.

Carolyn, who was to be co-pilot, lost all sense of being responsible for any flying. The flying was in Dad's hands and this was Dad's problem, not hers. Dad had checked the weather, made the flight plan, did the preflight checks and all the other details. Carolyn later said she was rubbing a nut on the bottom of the instrument panel, figuring as long as she could feel the nut, she was still alive.

Clara was calling out to God for mercy and help.

Mary had flown so many hours of her young life that she had learned to sleep well in the airplane. It helped pass the time. She had slept peacefully through one of our most eventful and dramatic flights. She must have had her seatbelt very tight.

I still could not find any of the shoreline check points I had marked on the map before the flight. So I picked one point on the shore line and did a 180° turn. I flew back along the shore to another point on the shoreline. I decided that just flying on and on without being able to locate myself on the map would only make matters much worse.

That was the longest time for feeling horrendous fear in all our forty-some years of flying. At other times I have had moments of intense fear, but this was the most nerve wracking.

– Clara

As I flew back and forth from point A to point B and amid all the turbulence and low ceiling, I tried to figure out where I was.

We must have flown back and forth for forty-five minutes until I recognized that just outside Bella Coola there was a fork in the inlet. I found my two points on the north shore of the southern inlet. I had marked several points on the north shore of the southern inlet before departure. So now at least I knew where we were.

All this time I was hoping the ceiling would not come down on the water. I was looking at the side of the mountain, wondering how it would be to try to land up the mountainside and let the airplane slide backwards down the mountain a few feet, hoping the trees would catch us. At least we would be alive.

Old pilots always say, "If the engine quits over the trees, land as slow and flat as possible. The tops of the trees have much give in them, so you will always walk away." I never practised that type of landing, because it would be too expensive! I knew several fellow pilots who had had to land in the tree tops. They all walked away from the crash. Could I do it upwards on a mountain slope? I was just hoping the engine would not quit, because landing on those huge waves would be fatal for all aboard. The mountain slope would have provided a better choice if ground fog moved towards us just above the waves.

Later Dad told us that it took all his energy and focus to keep the plane flying.
— Sharon

I was becoming exhausted. Looking at my map, I knew we could not go back to Bella Coola, because I was sure the weather had closed in there. Yet I knew that Bella Bella was forecasted to be clear all day when I had talked with Aviation Weather Services.

I looked for a flat area of trees and found one on the map three miles ahead on the south side of the inlet. I headed for that flat spot, and for the first time in my years of flying, I planned to land in the trees, camp out and let Search and Rescue find us. There is only so much stress one can take over a prolonged period of time.

*"Save us
from utter
destruction,"
Cathie kept
saying over
and over.
— Clara*

So I headed south for one minute and followed the southern shoreline. I kept scanning for the flat area ahead on my left, since we were flying west. Also, I told the others my plan to land in the trees on that flat area. "Landing in the trees on a flat area would be safer than trying to do it on trees on the mountain slope," I exclaimed.

Within a few minutes we reached the flat area and as we approached it, we could see sunshine ahead! When I saw the sunshine, I decided to go on to Bella Bella and not land in the trees. Shortly we were in the clear and there

*This is better
than the
Hardy Boys.
— Sharon*

was hardly any wind. We were out of the inlet over the Pacific Ocean. Eight minutes later we landed at Bella Bella, one happy bunch.

Of course the people at Bella Bella and Bella Coola were phoning each other to see if we had arrived at one of the places. "Where have you been?" they asked.

I sat on a tree stump and told them our story. They were glad we were safe and we were relieved the flight was over.

Later I heard that during that very hour, my mother, living almost 3000 miles away, had a strong urge to pray for our family because "they are going in the water." She spent one hour on her knees praying for us, but she had no idea what the problem was. She just pleaded with God to help us. After one hour, she had peace. The next time I phoned my mother, she asked where we had been going on that certain day at that certain hour. As I explained it to her, she just praised God for how He had prompted her to pray and that she was obedient.

Life Lesson *I BELIEVE IN THE POWER OF PRAYER AND IN BEING FAITHFUL TO GOD'S PROMPTINGS. GOD IS AWESOME! GODLY MOTHERS ARE WONDERFUL AND AWESOME TOO.*

• • •

The winter after Cathie married Sam Gingerich, they wanted to go along on a three-week seminar trip to British Columbia and Alaska in the Seneca II. Clara and I were pleased to have them along. Sam and Cathie added their dimension to the seminars by singing duets. They also dialogued about proper courtship, inexpensive weddings and the adjustments during the first year of marriage.

We began the first day of the trip by leaving Dryden, Ontario, about 8:30 a.m. Prior to loading, we weighed everything. The weight and balance was within limits. The luggage was loaded into the proper compartments. Then I checked the fuel and other preflight items. The flight to Lethbridge, Alberta, for a fuel stop was uneventful and the weather was beautiful as we crossed the prairies. After refueling, I checked the weather and winds for the remainder of the trip. I made the flight plan for a 10:30 a.m. departure at 12,000 feet out of Lethbridge for Kamloops, British Columbia.

The first ministry stop on this particular trip was Kamloops, British Columbia, to help with a Youth Seminar. The Sonrise Gospel Band had invited Clara and me to be the speakers during their music concerts.

When inquiring about the weather, I learned that light icing conditions were reported in the clouds. I chose a route that would cross the lowest mountains, because I wanted to be able to maintain a safe altitude on one engine in case of an engine failure.

I flight-planned from Lethbridge to Firni Intersection, to Kelowna over Skookum and on to Kamloops. I was pilot-in-command since I was the only one with IFR rating. We departed and climbed up to 12,000 feet and levelled off. As we started over the mountains, the clouds began to appear and then thicken. Now and then there were traces of light ice, but it was nothing to worry about.

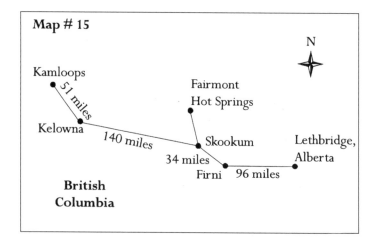

The clouds thickened until we were in a solid cloud layer and the light ice began to accumulate. The outside temperature was -20°F and I was becoming concerned.

"Edmonton Centre, this is Seneca II C-GRTH at 12,000 feet with a request," I radioed.

"C-GRTH, go ahead with your request," they replied.

"Edmonton Centre, RTH. We are in a solid cloud layer and picking up some ice. Requesting 11,000 feet."

"RTH, Edmonton Centre. You are cleared down to 11,000 feet," replied Edmonton Centre.

"Edmonton Centre, RTH cleared down to 11,000 feet."

On the descent to 11,000 feet the cloud layer looked brighter and thinner. The ice stopped accumulating and began to slowly dissipate, which was a relief. In my weather briefing, I had learned that the forecast for Skookum was clear skies and a temperature of 36°F.

By this time we were past the halfway point. If any clouds and icing showed up at the 11,000 feet, I felt confident we could make Fairmont Hot Springs where the sky was clear and the temperature was above freezing.

The Seneca II was equipped for flying in known ice conditions, but even at that, ice can build up in unprotected areas of the airframe and reduce the airspeed as well as increase the airplane weight. Additionally, the ice buildup would also affect the air flow and lift over certain parts of the wings which, in turn, increases the stalling speed.

As we flew along at 11,000 feet, the clouds thickened again and the ice began to accumulate. I could tell the airspeed was decreasing a few knots as the minutes passed by. I estimated we had another twelve minutes of flying before we would enter the airspace over the valley around Skookum, where we would be able to request a landing at Fairmont Hot Springs.

The ice continued to accumulate over unprotected areas of the airframe and the airspeed continued to decrease, but it was still safe. I also knew the stall speed was increasing. When the airspeed slows down near the increased stalling speed, we would begin to descend whether we wanted to or not!

The weather near Skookum was much worse than had been forecasted, so we were all trusting that we could make the last three minutes into the clear weather where I could request an immediate descent into the Fairmont area for a landing.

The airspeed continued to decrease and I calculated the difference between the airspeed and stalling speed which was about forty knots. That still left some margin for safety, but the situation was becoming alarming. Clara and Cathie clearly knew what a predicament we were in. Cathie explained our situation to Sam. I did more calculations and found the difference between our airspeed and our stalling speed to be thirty knots. That is a position no pilot wants to find himself in. But for us, the clouds and icing conditions over the Rocky Mountains were considerably worse than forecasted at the time of flight planning. There were no other airplanes at those altitudes to report actual conditions.

I am thankful we have someone to call on. This brings tears.
— Cathie

We had no way to know for sure what we were going into. There were airplanes up at 33,000 feet, but their reports did not help us.

One and a half minutes later we came into clear skies and I immediately requested a descent clearance from Edmonton Centre. Once cleared, I began a rapid descent into warmer temperatures. As we descended, the ice began to evaporate. At 5000 feet above the airport the temperature gauge showed 33°F and the ice began to peel off. We landed without incident at Fairmont Hot Springs.

Once in the airport terminal we were able to rest and allow our adrenaline to stabilize. Then I checked the weather for the remainder of the flight to Kamloops and it was forecasted to be good. In fact, the weather was clear for the next three weeks. Amazing!

Life Lesson   THE WORDS OF MY FATHER CAME BACK TO ME, "DO YOUR BEST AND GOD WILL DO THE REST."

• • •

We were flying from Calgary, Alberta, to Winnipeg, Manitoba, with the Seneca II. It was an eastbound IFR flight at 11,000 feet. We were in a solid cloud layer when the right vacuum pump went out. *No problem*, I thought. *We have two: left and right.*

I checked things over, and everything was functioning fine on the left vacuum pump. In my mind I was making plans how and where to have another vacuum pump installed in Winnipeg when, suddenly, the left vacuum pump went out. I couldn't believe it! The possibility of two vacuum pumps going out only minutes apart is almost nil. They are on two separate engines. But it happened.

Some of the critical instruments for IFR flying were gone and the autopilot disconnected. I was back to flying the basic ball and needle turn and bank indicator. The ball and needle instrument is a basic instrument used to keep the wings level. It is one of the first instruments all new pilots learn to use. As pilots, we tend to become used to the more advanced instruments and seldom use the ball and needle. This time I had no choice but to hand fly with very limited instrumentation. I had to keep the wings level, maintain 11,000 feet and keep the correct heading.

Once I knew everything was stabilized, I radioed, "Winnipeg Centre, this is C-GRTH at 11,000 feet."

"RTH, Winnipeg Centre," they replied.

"Winnipeg Centre, RTH. We just lost both vacuum pumps. Can you give me the weather for Yorkton, Saskatchewan?" I asked.

"RTH standby." Soon Winnipeg came back with, "Yorkton is scattered at 7000 feet."

"Could I have a clearance from present position direct Yorkton with descent to 6000 feet?" I inquired.

"RTH cleared present position direct Yorkton and cleared down to 6000," Winnipeg stated.

"Winnipeg Centre, RTH cleared present position direct Yorkton and down to 6000 feet," I acknowledged.

"Clara, tune in the Yorkton radios. I have my hands full flying this baby with only limited instrumentation and with the autopilot disconnected," I exclaimed. She followed my instructions. She was well trained for her tasks.

As soon as the Yorkton radios were tuned in, I followed that track and slowly descended to 6000 feet. The words from one of my instructors rang in my head, "Stay cool, no quick moves and use very gentle movements." Before long we were in the clear at 6800 feet.

"Winnipeg Centre, RTH is now in the clear at 6800 feet and cancelling IFR. Will proceed VFR," I said.

"RTH, Winnipeg Centre, check you at 6800 feet cancelling IFR," was their reply.

We proceeded VFR to Yorkton where we stayed overnight. Our plan had been to stop for fuel in Winnipeg and then fly on to Dryden. However, the weather forecast in Winnipeg for the

Life Lesson LIVE LIFE WITHOUT EXCESSIVE WORRY, BUT ALWAYS BE PREPARED FOR THE UNEXPECTED. WHEN THE UNEXPECTED HAPPENS, STAY CALM, DON'T PANIC, BE GENTLE BUT DIRECTIVE UNTIL THE UNEXPECTED IS PROCESSED AND BROUGHT TO A REASONABLE CONCLUSION. THEN GIVE YOURSELF TIME TO RELAX AND REGROUP.

rest of the day was not good. Also, I needed some time to allow my adrenaline to settle.

The next day the weather was clear. We flew VFR to Dryden uneventfully. The mechanics replaced both vacuum pumps before the next flight which was scheduled for the following week.

•   •   •

"You are a fortunate man," the mechanic said to me the morning I had just returned from a long flight from Alaska one night.

I had taken a commercial flight to Alaska to bring the Seneca II home after the new Seneca III engines had been installed. As you may remember, the engines had to be replaced after the gear up landing at Anaktuvuk Pass.

Before I made the final payment, the mechanic had me do a run-up and a test flight. After the test flight, I watched him remove the cowling and do an inspection of the engines for any oil leaks or anything unusual. All looked well to him and to me, so he replaced the cowlings and the final settlement was made.

Then I got fuel, checked the weather, made the flight plan and began my long night time trip from Alaska to Dryden with two fuel stops. The engines purred all through the night flight. I was a happy man with those new engines.

"Why am I a fortunate man?" I enquired of the mechanic.

"Well," he said, "I just removed the engine cowlings and the one gas line connection is leaking and gas is dripping onto the exhaust manifold. The one connection nut is loose. I am very surprised you didn't have a fire on your way home!" That statement sent all kinds of scenarios through my mind. What would I have done up at 21,000 feet if a fire would have started? I would have shut down that engine and closed the shut off fuel valve but whether or not that would have stopped the fire is an unknown.

After standing there for a few minutes in shock, disbelief and horror, I finally said, "Thank God I am here!" In my heart I had to renew my trust in mechanics even though, like the rest of us, they too can make mistakes. It became so clear to me again that much of life is putting trust in others.

Life Lesson   THE TRUST FACTOR IS SO VITAL IN MANY AREAS OF LIFE. ONE MUST ALLOW OTHERS TO MAKE MISTAKES THAT COULD PROFOUNDLY AFFECT ONE'S LIFE OR EVEN END ONE'S LIFE.

12

FLYING ABOVE
THE CLOUDS

By the year 2000 we were travelling frequently in the Arctic Regions from Nome, Alaska, to Nuuk, Greenland. The Seneca II was a good airplane, but aviation gasoline was becoming harder to purchase in the Arctic. Piston engines and extreme cold temperatures do not work well together.

The Seneca II was sold, and a twin turbo-prop Piper Cheyenne II was purchased. The Cheyenne II seemed to be the best airplane for flying long distances over mostly uninhabited country. It was the ideal airplane to buy for Arctic flying. Also, the Cheyenne II landing gear seemed to be very tough and durable.

We were able to buy a 1976 model with low airframe time for a reasonable price. The engines had been recently overhauled at the factory by Pratt and Whitney.

Learning to fly the Cheyenne II was a challenge. Chuck Bourne, a friend of ours from Kamloops, British Columbia,

who was an experienced Cheyenne II pilot, came to Dryden
for several weeks to prepare me for the IFR and the twin turbo-
prop pressurized flight test. I passed on my second attempt.
Chuck Bourne has been our aviation consultant and ad-
visor ever since. We are a private operation and not for hire, but
we still come under the commerical/business Canadian Aircraft Regulations. This means higher standards, more reports
and audits. The up side of this is that it helps keep me safer and
more knowledgeable.

The Cheyenne II has done well for us, and we can fly
long distances and altitudes up to 29,000 feet. My preferred altitudes are 23,000 eastbound and 24,000 westbound. At these
altitudes, one can fly above most of the bad weather.

The turbine engines do well in cold temperatures and
high altitudes. The colder it is, the better they perform. Turbine fuel is available at almost every airport in the Arctic. An
additional advantage is that the cabin is pressurized. We arrive at our destination less tired, and my wife's feet no longer
swell when we fly. We are very thankful for the Cheyenne
II.

One time while flying to Upernavik, Greenland, the airport weather reports worsened. However, up at 21,000 feet the
sun was shining. When we approached Upernavik, the radio
operator reported weather on the edge of IFR landing mini-
mums. I calculated that we had four hours of fuel and a one
and a half hour flight to our alternate airport at Sondre Stromfjord, where there was good weather.

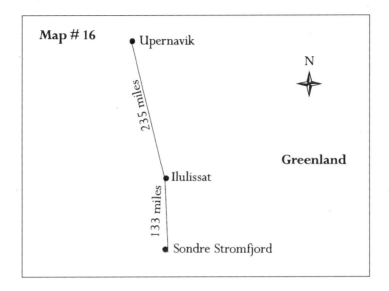

Map # 16
Upernavik
N
235 miles
Ilulissat
Greenland
133 miles
Sondre Stromfjord

I opted to try an IFR approach into Upernavik because a group of people were eager for the workshop. I committed myself to a missed approach if necessary. I thought that it would be necessary, but since we had plenty of fuel and no reported icing conditions, there was a ten percent chance we would be able to land.

The airport radio operator said it looked a little better to the northeast. Since the wind favoured landing towards the southwest, perhaps our final approach path would permit us to land.

I flew the approach pattern and entered the final approach path in solid cloud. The minimum descent altitude was 600 feet above the runway. As I flew the final approach path down to 600 feet, there was no sight of the runway or the airport. To the right, I could see the community of Upernavik and the Davis Straits. I turned right into the clear out over the

Davis Straits and then climbed up to 4000 feet into solid cloud again. The airport operator said the weather to the northeast looked even better, but over the airport it was still foggy.

Believing the low clouds might shift while I set up for and did another approach, I opted to try again. We still had plenty of fuel for Sondre Stromfjord.

On the second try, I had a brief glimpse of the runway as I pushed full power to do a missed approach again. The glimpse was too little and too late. We climbed back up to 4000 feet again and did some slow holding patterns over the navigational beacon, planning the next move.

The radio operator said that weather conditions to the northeast were still improving. I opted to try a third and final approach. Unknown to us, four people were at the airport waiting to pick us up. They had found a back room and were praying desperately for us to be able to land this time, because they really wanted the seminar.

I set up for and did the IFR approach procedures at the designated headings and altitudes. On the final approach path we saw nothing at 1000 feet, nor 900 feet, nor 800 feet, nor 700 feet, nor 600 feet. I was watching out the left side and Clara was looking out the right side. I was also watching the stop watch for my missed approach time. At 600 feet I saw nothing and time was up.

The muscles in my right arm tightened to push the throttles forward for another missed approach when Clara shouted, "There's the runway!" I quickly looked over and saw an open path to the runway. The runway markings were very clear and the airport environment was in sight for a safe landing. I pulled back the power, dropped full flaps and landed. As we were taxiing in, the clouds moved in again. We could not see the small colourful terminal building, so we followed the runway lights to the terminal.

The radio operator met us at the plane and said, "I am so glad you are here safely. There were four people in the back room praying that you would be able to land." Then he explained where to park. His men came with the fuel truck and another truck to take our luggage to our friends' vehicle.

When we walked into the terminal, the four very happy people met us with hugs. We had a great week there with those wonderful people.

Dad, I keep choking up and have tears in my eyes as I read these stories.

– Mary

13

"CRASHING"
IN THE SIMULATOR

Because we were flying in some of the most difficult areas and conditions in the Arctic with a Cheyenne II, I decided to go to Flight Safety International (FSI) every year for three and one-half days of recurrency training. Their slogan is, "The best part of an airplane is a well-trained pilot."

I will continue to go every year for recurrency training in theory and to practise flying in a state-of-the-art flight simulator. Trainers fly with me in our Cheyenne II as well.

The first time I went to FSI, I could not become accustomed to the flight simulator. It was not an airplane! They insisted that it flies similar to an airplane, but to me it was a toy machine. I kept "crashing." The good thing about "all going blank and black" in a simulator is that the instructor behind you, who is sitting in front of a vast panel of buttons and switches, suddenly turns on all the lights. It was not a real crash. It just felt the same as one.

For me as a pilot's wife, this is crucial. As I have flown with Clair, not only did his IFR training affect his personality, but the FSI training did too. It has made him a far safer and more confident pilot. But it also affects how he hears me and listens to my feelings, ideas and fears.
— Clara

The next time I returned to FSI for recurrency training, I learned to fly the simulator. I didn't crash once! Now I enjoy the simulator part of the training. It makes me feel, as a pilot, that I am flying the airplane. The instructors can also test me on many types of emergency procedures.

Clara has been going with me to FSI where she has been permitted to sit in the classes with me. Additionally, the instructors have wanted her to be in the right seat in the simulator because she is with me in the cockpit during ninety-five percent of my flying ever since all our daughters left home and married.

During her flight training, Clara passed the written exam with a mark of ninety-five percent. She also has her radio operator's license. She likes communicating on the radios as well as operating the GPS and tuning in the other navigational aids.

This time my knees did not knock, because I knew if I crashed in the simulator, I wouldn't hurt anything. The first time in the simulator, I did go off the runway.
— Clara

In August 2005 FSI convinced Clara that she needed to take their Confidence Builder's Course. She enjoyed that course, but when it came time to "fly" the Cheyenne II simulator, she was hesitant. After some discussion, she consented to twelve hours of simulator training over a two-year period.

Now, with the coaching of the simulator instructor in the back at the master control panel, Clara has safely landed the Cheyenne II!

Their logic for this was, that if she were ever in the right seat when the pilot collapsed, she could navigate to the closest suitable airport and safely land, especially if some pilot on the ground could talk with her on the radio during the landing process. With time, however, she will be able to do it without any coaching.

To say the least, the FSI instructors were proud of her, and so was I.

Life Lesson THE MORE THINGS A MARRIED COUPLE CAN DO TOGETHER, THE RICHER AND STRONGER WILL BE THEIR RELATIONSHIP.

14

THE FINAL FLIGHT—
GOING HOME

I am made for more than this world—much more! "He has set eternity in their hearts" (Ecclesiastes 3:11). I am made for another world. I am made for heaven where there will be:

– no more "Get that nose down!"
– no more turbulence
– no more icing conditions
– no more simulators
– no more emergencies
– no more accidents
– no more engine failures
– no more human errors
– no more gear-up landings
– no more missed approaches
– no more bad weather
– no more recurrencies

The Final Preflight Checklist is important for a successful flight that takes me to my desired destination. For this Final Flight I need to check for:

- unforgiven grudges
- unmade apologies
- praises to be given
- angry actions that need attention
- wrongs to be made right
- acceptance of imperfections
- unconfessed sins (I John 1:9)
- belief in Jesus (John 3:16)

This is powerful. A beautiful analogy.
— Clara

The more honestly I face my emptiness, chaos, trauma and confusion, the more I will become aware of a Holy Space within. It is a God-vacuum that only He can fill. The more I am in touch with the Holy Space, the easier it is for Him to lead me to where I really want to be—in the Heavenly Eden where there is perfect peace and harmony forever. It is a place where every desire and longing of my heart will be filled to the brim and running over with joy forever.

THE FINAL START-UP

My heart needs hope and trust in something bigger and beyond myself and this world. My courage for the journey moves me forward. Faith and love . . . spring from the hope that is stored up for us in heaven (see Colossians 1:4,5). I can handle the pressures of this life better because of the promise of better things to come. This world is not my permanent home. This world is only a preparation for my Final Flight to Glory. Death itself releases my spirit and soul to soar to heaven. We are made for more than this world. "He has also set eternity in the hearts of men . . ." (Ecclesiastes 3:11 NIV) We are made for Heaven!

Heaven is more than pudgy little babies with wings floating on fluffy clouds. If my picture of heaven is to move me, it must be a moving picture. So I go ahead and dream using my imagination. I picture the best ending to my story I can, and if that isn't heaven, something better is. When the Apostle Paul says, "No eye has seen, no ear has heard, no mind has conceived what God has prepared for those who love him" (1 Corinthians 2:9 NIV), he simply means I cannot outdream God about how wonderful heaven is. At the end of my personal journey, there is something beyond my wildest imagination.

There is in the heart of every man, woman and child an inconsolable longing for **intimacy**, for **beauty** and for **adventure**. That is what Heaven has to offer to all who believe. ". . . whoever believes in him shall not perish but have eternal life . . ." (John 3:16 NIV).

THE FINAL FLIGHT

The door on which I have been knocking all my life will finally be opened.

"For the Lord himself will come down from heaven, with a loud command, with the voice of the archangel and with the trumpet call of God, and the dead in Christ will rise first. After that we who are still alive . . . will be caught up . . . in the clouds to meet the Lord in the air. And so we will be with the Lord forever" (I Thessalonians 4:16, 18 NIV). This will be jet propulsion beyond my best imagination. Up there will be exotic, spiritual beauty and emotional fulness beyond my wildest expectations.

The Final Landing

This will be that final landing into the arms of Jesus where I can enjoy Him and He will enjoy me for all eternity!

THE END

•   •   •

I love this last chapter. A beautiful fit to a beautiful book. I'm proud of you, Dad.   — *Sharon*

Wow, I really enjoyed the whole book, Dad.
                                          — *Mary*

I like it, Dad. Very interesting. I liked the whole book.
                                          — *Cathie*

Clara and Judy during flight training.

Sharon learning about engines during training.

Mary, Cathie and Carolyn on a family trip during their training.

Schnupp family in their home on Beaver Lake, Dryden, Ontario, Canada around the time the older girls did their flight training.

Five members of the Schunpp family preparing to leave from the lake by their home to a northern community for family life teaching.

Cathie, Clair, Duane and Clara replacing the front oil seal and cleaning the engine on the Piper Seneca II.